ORDERING
YOUR
PRIVATE
WORLD

ORDERING
YOUR
PRIVATE
WORLD

REVISED AND UPDATED

Gordon MacDonald

W PUBLISHING GROUP

AN IMPRINT OF THOMAS NELSON

Published in Nashville, Tennessee, by W Publishing Group, an imprint of Thomas Nelson.

Thomas Nelson titles may be purchased in bulk for educational, business, fund-raising, or sales promotional use. For information, please e-mail SpecialMarkets@ThomasNelson.com.

ISBN 978-0-7180-8800-2 (trade paper)
ISBN 978-0-7180-8808-8 (eBook)

Library of Congress Cataloging-in-Publication Data

MacDonald, Gordon, 1939–
Ordering your private world / Gordon MacDonald—Rev. ed.
p. cm.
Includes bibliographical references.
ISBN 10: 0-7852-6381-0 (hardcover)
ISBN 13: 978-0-7852-6381-4 (hardcover)

1. Christian life. I. Title.
BV4501.3 .M23 2003
248.4—dc21
2002012547

Printed in the United States of America

19 20 21 LSC 8 7 6 5

CONTENTS

CONTENTS

If a (person) has not order within him,
He cannot spread order about him.
—Ezra Pound

AUTHOR'S NOTE

MANY YEARS AGO I WROTE A BOOK ABOUT THE INTERIOR LIFE OF THE Christ-follower and called it *Ordering Your Private World*. Some people read it and spoke of its candor and practicality.

OPW—my nickname for the book—began with the suggestion that many people who call themselves Christians pay scant attention to the state of their souls and, as a result, end up experiencing disappointment with their journey of faith. In a later edition of *OPW*, I recounted an unforgettable day in my own life when I had to acknowledge my own spiritual shallowness. In the early pages of this book I will retell the story.

Much of my inspiration began with the words of John the Baptizer, who'd been influenced by the thinking of the Old Testament prophet Isaiah.

> "Prepare [put into order] the way for the Lord,
>   make straight paths for him.
> Every valley shall be filled in,
>   every mountain and hill made low.
> The crooked roads shall become straight,
>   the rough ways smooth.
> And all people will see God's salvation." (Luke 3:4–6 NIV)

What I heard John (and Isaiah) saying was: *If you have a desire to experience God's order in your life, you will have to begin at the heart—or soul level—this deepest part of us that I like to call the private world.*

What I wish I'd made clearer when I wrote the first *OPW* was that I was not trying to promote some new spiritual life curriculum. Rather, I wanted the reader to ask: *How have the great champions of many Christian generations kept themselves fresh and in touch with the voice of the living God?*

One hundred years ago, Oswald Chambers made the point this way:

> The battle is lost or won in the secret places of the will before God, never first in the external world. . . . Nothing has any power over the [person] who has fought out the battle before God and won there. . . . I must get the thing settled between myself and God in the secret places of my soul where no stranger intermeddles, and *then I can go forth* with the certainty that the battle is won.[1]

So here I am again, now an aging man, a grandfather five times, seventy-eight years old. I am still challenged—every day!—by the notion of ordering my private world. And I'd like to offer a rewritten, more personal, even a bit autobiographical *OPW* that will catch you up on what I've learned over all these years.

—GORDON MACDONALD
CONCORD, NEW HAMPSHIRE

PREFACE

The Day I Hit the Wall

I DID NOT COME FROM MY MOTHER'S WOMB AS A NATURALLY ORDERED person.

As a child, I rarely put my toys and books away, and when I got a bit older, I often left my bike in places where my father was sure to run over it with his car when he came home for dinner.

During my teen years, the people who hired me for afterschool jobs were critical of my work ethic. Not thorough, they said of me.

I disappointed girlfriends when I neglected to buy valentines, birthday gifts, and prom corsages.

As a young twentysomething male, I rarely put away my clothes, frequently misplaced my car keys and wallet, and usually failed to leave the bathroom in the condition that I'd found it.

Throughout my school years, teachers complained that I was easily distracted, a daydreamer, scatterbrained. One wrote on my report card, "While Gordon may be physically present in the classroom, his mind is usually somewhere else—which is a shame because it might be a better mind if it stayed right here."

One day in my teen years, a frustrated church youth leader pushed me into a corner and said through clenched teeth, "When are you ever going to grow up?" He added a few more comments about my squandered potential, my lack of dependability, and my childish behavior, then stalked off. I got sick of hearing about this so-called potential of mine.

I don't think I was ever spiritually ordered either. Having been church-centered all my life (my father was a pastor), I knew all the Bible stories and had committed scads of Scripture verses to memory. I regularly won Sunday school perfect attendance certificates and pins. But none of this led to unusual conduct or character formation that someone would equate with being a serious Christ-follower (a term I prefer to *Christian*).

Now, it wasn't that I was such a bad person in the early days of my life. To borrow the words of the Revelation writer, I was neither hot nor cold . . . just kind of lukewarm. Average. Mediocre. Unimpressive.

So it was that I lived in a general pattern of disorder in both my private world and my public one for the first twenty-plus years of my life.

Then came a time in the onset of adulthood when my irresponsible ways began to result in increasingly serious consequences, and I saw that if I didn't bring a better order to my private world, the future would not be promising.

One Saturday morning in my thirtieth year, an event occurred that changed my life. I have often spoken and written about what happened that morning because it was then that I was jolted—really jolted!—into a recognition of a huge and hidden part of myself to which I'd never paid adequate attention: my soul . . . or what I like to call my private world.

It had been seven years since Gail and I had married. Graduate school was behind me, and we were the parents of two children. I was the youngish pastor of a wonderful midsized church that was growing. I had this sense that Gail and I were on our way to fulfilling all of our early dreams. What we'd talked about so enthusiastically during the early years of our lives together seemed as if it was becoming a reality.

I had accumulated a few months of busyness (*I mean really busy!*) in my work. Now, there is a busyness that reflects a plan of activity, a pattern of priorities, and a sense of purposefulness. It is a good and satisfying busyness through which one grows and increases competence. But there is also a busyness (a destructive busyness, actually) that reflects a chaotic way of life—a way of doing in which one is simply responding to the next thing in the day. *The next thing!* It makes no difference whether it has significance; it's just the next thing, and one does it because it's *there* to do.

In that thirtieth year I was swept along in that second kind of busyness, much like someone being swept along in the rapids of a raging river. Out of control. Fearful of capsizing. Feeling quite unprotected.

For several months I had been living the 24/7 routine, as they say, doing the work of an ambitious, anxious-to-prove-himself organizational leader. There had been many public speaking events, funerals, weddings, counseling sessions, planning discussions, and trouble-shooting meetings. There seemed to be an endless stream of people who wanted a piece of me. And the only way I knew how to respond to all these demands was to keep saying, "Yes, yes, yes . . . no problem . . . consider it done . . . glad to serve . . ." to all of them. "No" didn't appear in my vocabulary.

And the result of all this hurry?

The incessant work, that inky mood, those destabilizing thoughts had done nothing but drain me: spiritually, emotionally, intellectually, and physically. *Drained* is certainly the operative word, and it was a surprising sensation because, like most young adults, I assumed that energy and vitality were boundless and inexhaustible. My mind was continually racing trying to keep ahead of everyone. My emotions were oversensitive to the complaints and criticisms of people. Physically, I was getting out of shape, and I felt perpetually unrested. Most of all—though I didn't appreciate it—my soul (the small part of it of which I was aware) had become clogged and cluttered. Jesus seemed very distant. I could preach about Him, pray publicly to Him, but it didn't mean there was any sense of closeness.

I have to add, there was scant time for Gail, our children, or the few people I considered friends. Looking back, I realize that I was offering a "downgraded Gordon" to those closest to me: tired, irritable, and critical.

And now, as I said at the beginning, it was Saturday. I came rushing down the stairs of our home that day and entered the kitchen, where Gail was preparing breakfast for the family.

"I have to skip breakfast," I said as I put on my coat. "Got to get to the office. I'm behind on my preparation for tomorrow's sermon. Oh, and a couple of staff members want to meet me for lunch to talk about a problem they've got. So I probably won't be back till—"

"You do what you have to do," Gail interrupted, "but on your way out the door, you might want to think about the fact that you haven't spent any meaningful hours with the children lately. For that matter, you and I haven't had much time to ourselves either."

I froze as I tried to decide how to respond.

But before anything came to me, Gail spoke again. "Tell me, Gordon: Do you really want to live this way? Is this what you want the coming years to be like? Is this the kind of life we agreed to when we got married?"

Gail's questions stopped me cold. I should have immediately responded, "No! I don't want to live this way." But then I would have had to explain why that was exactly what I was doing: *living that way*.

And I began to cry. Not a few tears and not for a short while.

I cried for at least four hours . . . great, wrenching sobs that came from near, as best I can figure, the bottomless pit of my soul.

I remember turning away quickly when I heard the children coming down the stairs behind me. It was bad enough that Gail was witnessing this onset of my tears. But the children too?

I rushed to the living room, threw myself on the couch, and ended up weeping nonstop for the entire morning. And just when I thought the tears might stop, they started again. It was rather scary.

Such an explosion of emotion had never happened to me before. *Is this what they call a breakdown?* I remember asking myself. Did I need a doctor, a hospital? Why had no one ever described a moment like this for me?

I heard Gail phone a neighbor and ask if our children could spend the morning with her. Then she came to where I was. Embracing me, she kept saying how much she loved me, assuring me that God was with us. Nothing more than that: no humiliating comments about men crying, no trying to fix me, no smug reminder that this was all my making—which it was. She just quietly entered into my experience.

I remember the morning in considerable detail. It was as though my inner being was like a basement filled with floodwaters. But this was raw emotion and whatever was behind it. And like a flooded basement, it needed to be pumped out. Thus, the wash of tears.

I have looked back many times, wondering what I was crying for that day. Perhaps it was some of the wounds and sorrows that had been handed down from father to son from previous generations. Then again, perhaps I was weeping for my own sadnesses, the ones I had lived through as a boy and never brought to resolution. What about the possibility that I was simply reflecting weeks and weeks of stressful life in which there had been no pause and no inner, spiritual maintenance? How about the chance that it was all of these possibilities?

That Saturday was the day I learned, the hard and frightening way, that I could not go on living the way I was living and expect to be a spiritual leader (or any other kind of leader) of people. I often refer to that morning as the day I hit the wall.

I had always wanted to be a pastor. My father had been one, and my grandfather, for all practical purposes, had been one. The call to pastoral life was in my blood, you could say, and with great anticipation I pointed in that direction throughout my younger years. Even as a young boy I could see myself someday in the pulpit. When a teenager, even when I lived in a bit of spiritual defiance, I knew there would come a moment when I would capitulate to the call of God and become what He had made me to be: *a pastor*, a spiritual shepherd to people.

My father, an inveterate teacher, had taught me almost everything there was to know about how to lead a church. Words had come easily to me from the earliest days. So had social skills. I knew how to engage with people, think quickly on my feet, see issues and problems from the biggest possible perspective. By nature, I was an idea man, a visionary of sorts, and I possessed an ability to persuade people to follow.

You call all of these things, or at least I do, *natural gifts* or talents. They come in the course of life to some people through our temperaments, our life experiences, and the influence of family and close friends. To a considerable extent, they were almost all the natural gifts I needed to get a very fast start in pastoral ministry.

When I use the term *fast start*, I am referring to those things that might (but shouldn't) dazzle a young, ambitious, impressionable man or woman of any vocation. Fast start fits with the vocabulary of *perceived success*: large numbers, big bucks, sudden victories, quick recognition, and meeting "important" people—things which

I see as rather insignificant today but in times past was tempted to take rather seriously.

This was what fast start meant for me. A Midwestern congregation of several hundred people had called me right out of seminary at the age of twenty-eight to be their pastor. And in the first couple of years almost everything I did turned out right. Well, not everything. But it seemed like that.

In addition to the natural giftedness I've mentioned, there were some other very practical reasons why this fast start happened. For example, I had a remarkably mature and insightful wife who put every bit of muscle (spiritual and otherwise) she had into my ministry and saved me from a thousand errors of judgment. Then, too, my predecessor had made some serious leadership mistakes, and that meant that almost everything I did, by contrast, the congregation viewed with favor and affection.

Humanly speaking, the future looked extremely bright, and even those who had tracked my life during my school days and had sometimes worried about whether I would amount to anything were beginning to think that I might be on to something special in the future. If ministry was all about natural talent, timely opportunities, and great assistance from those who loved you, I was on my way. *Natural gifts.* We all have them, I suppose, some of us having more than others. They can carry young men and women for a long distance. They certainly carried me.

Natural gifts such as personal charisma, mental brightness, emotional strength, and organizational ability can impress and motivate people for a long time. Sometimes they can be mistaken for spiritual vitality and depth. Sadly, we do not have a Christian culture today that easily discriminates between a person of spiritual depth and a person of raw talent. Like the wheat and the tares of Jesus' parable, they can be difficult to distinguish. The result is that more than a few people can be fooled into thinking they are being influenced by a spiritual giant when, in fact, they are being manipulated by a dwarf.

We must always be aware that there are leaders who can build great organizations (including churches) on natural gifts. Say the right words, be smart enough to do the right things, be insightful enough to connect with the right people, and one can go a long way before anyone ever discovers that the inner life is close to empty.

When my emotional deluge finally subsided, I remained where I was for the rest of the day seeking a clearer understanding of what had happened.

Jesus, I remember praying, *is there a message I'm supposed to get from this experience?* I prayed that prayer several times during the afternoon, and the answer that came back was yes—there was indeed a message that I dare not miss, lest the coming years of my life dissolve into a mess. When the message came—quiet words in my heart—it came suddenly, clearly, convincingly as if it were a text message from a friend. I have never forgotten it.

Now you know what it's like to live out of an empty soul.

That one sentence was the message!

An empty soul. What does it mean to have an empty soul?

My answer to my own question? A soul—our spiritual space—is empty when one tries to do soul-based things but makes little or no effort to keep that soul filled. It would be like trying to drive a high-performance car with an empty gas tank.

As this notion, that my soul might be dangerously empty and disorganized, tumbled about in my mind that afternoon, I began to appreciate for the first time how badly I had neglected this inner space.

The truth was that I had invested the early years of my adult Christ-following life enlarging that part of Gordon that was visible and potentially impressive to the world around me. I came to depend on talents, such as speaking well, being a people-pleaser, and charming people with my visions and my enthusiasm. In short, being a high-performance organizational leader.

I am ashamed to acknowledge that in those early years I gave people more of the spiffy leader and less the man Jesus intended me to be: deepening, loving, quiet-spirited, gentle.

By the end of that day you could say that I had gone through something of a conversion experience. I would deliberately reorder my life, I determined, and I would do my best to jump the track from a life and work based on natural giftedness to one built on discipline and intentionality. Or to put it in terms in keeping with the title of this book, I determined to *order my private world.*

In the hours that followed, I tried as best as I could to acknowledge to God my regret that I had misinterpreted the conduct of my life and the use of my natural gifts. I wanted Him to know that I desired to change and that if He would intervene in my spiritual journey and acquaint me with some new processes of discipline, I would listen as best as I could. What I was seeking—put in the biggest possible terms—was a renovation of my life.

Please don't entertain the notion that everything instantly changed. It didn't. I had lots of hard work to do. In fact, it would take years of hard work. I say "hard work" because the task of renovating, or reordering, one's private and public world is no small challenge.

And the job never quite gets done. I have now come to understand that there are issues that I will probably take to my grave.

If there was a first step for me in my life-renovation process, it began with a simple, spiral-bound notebook that I came to call a journal. I'd read about journals from time to time, how many of the great saints had kept them and passed on to later generations the stories of their inner and outer lives. And I'd taken note that some of the modern writers whom I admire had kept journals for many years.

In my journal, I began listing the things that had drained my private world:

- I'm living at too fast a speed.
- I am awash in too many choices, and I'm not good at saying no.
- I'm overwhelmed by the complexities of my organization.
- I compare myself to other people . . . and I always feel like I lose.
- I think that technology and talent can solve my problems, but they can't.
- I am tempted to think that all I have to do is preach to people and they will come around.
- I have not respected the force of the anti-faith culture I'm living in.
- I am not seeking times of deep reverence, prayer, in the presence of Jesus.

These admissions and others were not easy to make because they indicated a lack of order. As I noted earlier, I am not by nature an organized person. I do not pick up things automatically. I do not finish things before I start something else. I am not good with details. I can easily forget things I've promised to do. And I can get easily distracted. I am a daydreamer (having a very rich imagination). I can be very playful, and I can fall effortlessly into the trap of trying to please everybody. As you can imagine, there was a lot that needed renovating here.

More than once, people who have read an earlier version of *Ordering Your Private World* have come up to me and said, "It must be nice to organize your life so naturally." And they are always startled when I say to them, "*OPW* was not written by a naturally ordered man; it was written by a naturally *disordered* man who had to get his life in line if he was ever to amount to anything."

Most of the time they are encouraged by those words.

I must not conclude this preface without emphasizing one indispensable principle. The order of my private world is an inside-out matter, not an outside-in matter. We are all too tempted to buy gadgets with the hopes that they will bring tidiness of life. But it doesn't work that way. Forget the gadgets and start with the interior, the private world.

The order we seek begins with a thorough scouring of the inside of life. With tough questions that it may take others to help us answer. With a confronting of beliefs and principles that are toxic and destructive. With a listening to the voice of God who has better things for us.

Today I look back on that Saturday in the thirtieth year of my life—the day I hit the wall—as one of the most important days of my life journey. That was the day the warning sirens sounded, the day I saw all too clearly where I was headed if something did not change in my private world. It was the day I started the search for inner (and a resulting outer) orderliness. A process that continues until this day.

ONE

THE SINKHOLE SYNDROME

THE RESIDENTS OF A FLORIDA APARTMENT BUILDING AWOKE TO A TER-rifying sight outside their windows. The ground beneath the street in front of their building had literally collapsed, creating a massive depression that Floridians call a sinkhole. Tumbling into the ever-deepening pit were automobiles, pavement, sidewalks, and lawn furniture. The building itself would obviously be the next to go.

Sinkholes occur, scientists say, when underground streams drain away during seasons of drought, causing the ground at the surface to lose its underlying support. Suddenly everything simply caves in, leaving people with a frightening suspicion that nothing—not even the earth beneath their feet—is trustworthy.

There are many people whose lives are like one of Florida's sinkholes. It is likely that at one time or another many of us have perceived ourselves to be on the verge of a sinkhole-like cave-in. In the feelings of numbing fatigue, a taste of apparent failure, or the bitter experience of disillusionment about goals or purposes, we may sense something within us about to give way. We feel we are just a moment from a collapse that will threaten to sweep our entire world into a bottomless pit. Sometimes there seems to be little that can be done to prevent such a collapse. What is wrong?

If we think about it for very long, we may discover the existence of an inner space—our private world—about which we were formerly ignorant. I hope it will become apparent that, if neglected, this private world will not sustain the weight of events and stresses that press upon us.

Some people are surprised and disturbed when they make such a self-discovery. They suddenly realize that they have spent most of their time and energy establishing life on the visible level, at the surface. They have accumulated a host of good and perhaps even excellent assets such as academic degrees, work experience, key relationships, and physical strength or beauty.

There is nothing wrong with all of that. But often it is discovered almost too late that the private world of the person is in a state of disorderliness or weakness. And when that is true, there is always potential for the sinkhole syndrome.

We must come to see ourselves as living in two very different worlds. Our outer, or public world, is easier to deal with. It is much more measurable, visible, and expandable. Our outer world consists of work, play, possessions, and a host of acquaintances that make up a social network. It is the part of our existence easiest to evaluate in terms of success, popularity, wealth, and beauty. But our inner world is more spiritual in nature. Here is a center in which choices and values can be determined, where solitude and reflection might be pursued. It is a place for conducting worship and confession, a spot where the moral and spiritual pollution of the times need not penetrate.

Most of us have been taught to manage our public worlds well. Of course, there will always be the undependable worker, the poorly organized homemaker, and the person whose social capacities are so immature that he becomes a drain on everyone around him. But most of us have learned to take orders, make schedules, and give directions. We know which systems best suit us in terms of work and relationship. We choose proper forms of leisure and pleasure. We can choose friends and make those relationships work well.

Our public worlds are filled with a seeming infinity of demands on our time, our loyalties, our money, and our energies. And because these public worlds of ours are so visible, so real, we have to struggle to ignore all their seductions and demands. They scream for our attention and action.

But there is this private world in every one of us, a world that may be as infinite in size as we perceive our public worlds to be. But often the private world—like the depths of the ocean—remains unexplored, full of surprises, ambushes, emotions, and dreams.

In a past season of the popular television series *Survivor*, one of the finalists, Gerry, talked about the pressures she faced as she tried to avoid getting voted off the island. When asked if she had surprised herself in her drive to win the million-dollar prize, she said, "Honestly? I had no idea that this was going to be as tough as it is. I have woken up in the morning and gone through an entire day wondering who I am. Things come out of my mouth in frustration and hunger and . . . stress that, after they come out, I want to suck them back in because it's not the same thing I would normally say or [do] . . . so, yeah, I've surprised myself in a lot of ways."

Although Gerry describes life in a contrived (made-for-TV) world, she speaks like a fast-tracker. As life heats up, she seems amazed to discover traits of personal character that she really didn't want to own.

In a real world similar to Gerry's, there is a temptation to ignore the existence of our private world because it does not shout quite so loudly when neglected. It can be effectively shortchanged for large periods of time before it gives way to a sinkhole-like cave-in.

Oscar Wilde, author and playwright, was one who paid scant

attention to his private world. William Barclay quoted Wilde's confession:

> The gods had given me almost everything. But I let myself be lured into long spells of senseless and sensual ease. . . . Tired of being on the heights, I deliberately went to the depths in search for new sensation. What the paradox was to me in the sphere of thought, perversity became to me in the sphere of passion. I grew careless of the lives of others. I took pleasure where it pleased me, and passed on. I forgot that every little action of the common day makes or unmakes character, and that therefore what one has done in the secret chamber, one has some day to cry aloud from the house-top. I ceased to be lord over myself. I was no longer the captain of my soul, and did not know it. I allowed pleasure to dominate me. I ended in horrible disgrace.[1]

When Wilde wrote, "I was no longer the captain of my soul," he described a person whose inner world was in shambles, whose life was caving in. Although his words reach great heights of personal drama, they are similar to what many could say—many who, like him, have ignored their internal existence.

I believe that one of the great battlegrounds of our age is the private world of the individual. There is a contest that must be fought particularly by those who call themselves practicing or observant Christ-followers. Among them are those who work hard, shouldering massive responsibilities at home, at work, and at church. *They are good people, but they are very, very tired!* And, thus, they too often live on the verge of a sinkhole-like collapse. Why? Because although their worthwhile actions are very unlike those of Wilde, like him they become too public/world-oriented, ignoring the private side until it is almost too late.

Wayne Muller wrote:

The busier we are, the more important we seem to ourselves and, we imagine, to others. To be unavailable to our friends and family, to be unable to find time for the sunset (or even to know that the sun has set at all), to whiz through our obligations without time for a single mindful breath, this has become the model of a successful life.[2]

Our Western cultural values have helped to blind us to this tendency. We are naively inclined to believe that the most publicly active person is the most privately spiritual. We assume that the larger the church, the greater its heavenly blessing. The more information about the Bible a person possesses, we think, the closer he or she must be to God.

Because we tend to think like this, the temptation is to give imbalanced attention to our public worlds at the expense of the private. More programs, more meetings, more learning experiences, more relationships, more busyness; until it all becomes so heavy at the surface of life that the whole thing trembles on the verge of collapse. Fatigue, disillusionment, failure, defeat all become frightening possibilities. The neglected private world can no longer hold the weight.

I bumped into a man who had claimed Christian faith for several years. During our conversation, I asked him one of those questions that Christ-followers ought to ask one another but feel odd in doing so.

I said, "Tell me, how are you doing spiritually?"

He responded, "Interesting question! What's a good answer? Oh, I'm okay, I guess. I wish I could say I was growing or feeling closer to God. But the truth is that I'm sort of standing still."

He gave the impression of wanting to pursue the matter, and so I threw in another question.

"Are you taking time regularly to order your inner life?"

He looked at me inquisitively. If I had used an old Christian term such as, "How's your quiet time?" he would have known exactly how to answer. That would have been measurable, and he could have responded in terms of days, hours, and minutes, systems and techniques. But I had asked about the order of his inner life. And the key word is *order*, a word of *quality*, not quantity. Now he showed discomfort.

"When does a guy ever get to order his inner life? I've got work piled up to keep me going for the rest of the year. I'm out every night this week. My wife is after me to take a week's vacation. The house needs painting. So there's not too much time to think about 'ordering the inner life,' as you put it."

He paused for a moment and then asked, "What is the inner life anyway?"

Now that's a showstopper of a question. Think of it! Here is a professing Christ-follower who has "done church" for years, has gained a Christian reputation for doing Christian things, but has never pondered the possibility that, underneath all the action and well-meaning religious noise, there has got to be something solid, something dependable. The fact that he sees himself as too busy to maintain an inner world, and that he is not sure he knows what it is anyway, tells me that he may have missed, by a significant distance, the central point of a life in touch with God. You could say that we had a lot to talk about in the following hour.

Few people wrestled with the pressures of a public world more than Anne Morrow Lindbergh, wife of Charles, the famous aviator. And she jealously guarded her private world and wrote some insightful comments about it in her classic book *The Gift from the Sea*:

> I want first of all . . . to be at peace with myself. I want a single-ness of eye, a purity of intention, a central core to my life that will enable me to carry out these obligations and activities as well as I can. I want, in fact—to borrow from the language of the saints—to live "in grace" as much of the time as possible. I am not using this term in a strictly theological sense. By grace I mean an inner harmony, essentially spiritual, which can be translated into outward harmony. I am seeking perhaps what Socrates asked for in the prayer from the Phaedrus when he said, "May the outward and inward man be one." I would like to achieve a state of inner spiritual grace from which I could function and give as I was meant to in the eye of God.[3]

Fred Mitchell, once a leader in the world missionary movement, used to keep a motto on his desk that read, "Beware of the Barrenness of a Busy Life." He, too, understood the potential collapse that follows when the inner world is ignored.

———

The Florida sinkhole is a physical picture of a spiritual problem with which many Western Christ-followers must deal. As the pressure of life continues to grow, the lives of more people will resemble a sinkhole, unless they gaze inward and ask themselves, *Is there a private world beneath the noise and action at the surface? A world that needs to be explored and maintained? Can strength and resilience be developed that will bear up under the growing pressure at the surface?*

In a lonely moment in Washington when John Quincy Adams

was overwhelmed by homesickness for his Massachusetts family, he wrote them a letter, addressing comments of encouragement and counsel to each son and daughter. To his daughter he wrote about the prospect of marriage and the kind of man she should choose to marry. His words reveal how highly he regarded an ordered private world:

> Daughter! Get you an honest man for a husband and keep him honest. No matter whether he is rich, provided he be independent. Regard the honor and moral character of the man, more than all other circumstances. *Think of no other greatness but that of the soul, no other riches but those of the heart.*[4]

TWO

A VIEW FROM THE BRIDGE

A FRIEND WAS ONCE AN OFFICER ABOARD A UNITED STATES NAVY nuclear submarine. He related to me an experience that happened one day while the sub was on duty in the Mediterranean. Many ships were passing overhead on the surface, and the submarine was forced to make a large number of violent maneuvers to avoid possible collisions.

In the absence of the captain, my friend was duty officer, in charge of giving the commands by which the submarine was positioned at each moment. Because there was such a sudden and unusual amount of movement, the captain, who had been in his own quarters, suddenly appeared on the bridge asking, "Is everything all right?"

"Yes, sir!" was my friend's reply. The captain took a quick look around and then started back out through the hatch to leave the bridge. As he disappeared, he said, "It looks all right to me too." With just a few words and the abrupt exit, the captain conveyed his unqualified confidence in the duty officer's leadership.

That simple, routine encounter between a naval commander and one of his trusted officers provided me with a helpful picture of the order of one's private world. All around that submarine the potential danger of collision was lurking. It was enough to make any alert captain show concern. But that danger was outside. Down deep inside the sub was a quiet place where there could be absolute control of the ship's destiny. And that was where the captain instinctively headed.

On the bridge, the center of command, there was not a hint of panic, only a calm and deliberate series of actions being carried out by a highly trained crew of seamen doing their jobs. Thus, when the commander appeared on the bridge to assure himself that everything was in order, it was. "Is everything all right?" he asked. Assured that it was, he looked about and agreed, "It looks all right to me too." He had gone to the right place and received the proper answer.

That is how the captain organized his sub. The appropriate procedures were practiced a thousand times when there was no danger. Thus, when it was time for action in a precarious situation, there was no need for the captain to overreact. He could anticipate an excellent performance from the people on the bridge. When things are in order there, the submarine is secure no matter what the external circumstances. "It looks all right to me too," says the captain.

But there have been cases in which those procedures have been ignored, perhaps left unpracticed. Then there can be disaster. Then ships collide and sink, causing great loss.

And so it is with human life when there is disorganization on the "bridge" of the inner world. The accidents that occur there have names like *burnout, breakdown*, or *blowup*.

It is one thing for a person to make a mistake or even to fail. We learn our best lessons of procedure and character under such conditions. But it is another thing to watch human beings disintegrate before our very eyes because there were no resources of interior support in the midst of the pressure.

The *Wall Street Journal* once offered a series of articles entitled "Executive's Crisis," and one story featured Jerald H. Maxwell, a young entrepreneur who founded a hi-tech company and immediately led it to high profitability. For a while he was celebrated as a managerial genius. But, unfortunately, just for a while. A sudden downturn in the economy changed everything. The company's stock cratered, as they say, and the board of directors was forced to take drastic action:

> The day is etched into Jerald H. Maxwell's memory. His family will never forget it either. To them it is the day he started weeping in his room, the day his exuberant self-confidence ended and his depression began, the day his world—and theirs—came tumbling down.

Maxwell had been fired! Everything in his life seemed to fall apart, and he appeared to lack the inner resources to handle the situation. The *Journal* continued:

> For the first time in his life, Mr. Maxwell was a failure, and it shattered him. His feeling of defeat led to an emotional breakdown, gnawed away at the bonds between Mr. Maxwell and his wife and four sons and pushed him to the brink. "When things fell apart, they felt so bad I was ashamed," Mr. Maxwell recalls. He pauses and sighs, then goes on: "It says in the Bible that all you have to do is ask and you will receive. Well, I asked for death many times."[1]

Most of us have never wished for death as Maxwell did. But more than a few of us have experienced the same pressure from the outer world, crowding in on us to such an extent that we wondered if some sort of death would be desirable. During such moments, we ask ourselves about the strength of our reserves—whether we can keep going, whether it is worth it to keep pressing, whether it may be time to "cut and run." In short, we are not sure that there is enough spiritual, psychic, or physical energy to keep moving at the pace we are presently trying to maintain.

I've been where Maxwell was in his darkest hours. Our stories are a bit different, but the feelings are not. For a few hours, perhaps for a few days (for some a lot longer than that), there is a numbness. All the resolve is gone. Self-confidence disappears. It seems as if there will be no tomorrow.

It's in the moments that Jerald Maxwell faced, moments that I once knew, that one is forced to the very bottom of one's soul. Is there anything there? The answer to the question will be based on whether something has been stored there in better days.

Back to the submarine. Recall, once more, what the captain of that submarine did. When there was a sense of violent turbulence all around, he headed for the bridge to determine whether things were in order. The answer, he knew, would be found nowhere else. And if everything was all right there, he knew he could retire to his quarters with confidence. The ship could handle the turbulent circumstances if everything was all right on the bridge.

If you please, another sea incident. One of my favorite Bible stories tells of the afternoon Jesus' disciples found themselves in a raging storm on the Sea of Galilee. Soon they were terrified and had lost all composure. Here were men who had fished this sea for years, who had their own equipment, and who must have seen such storms before. But for some reason, this time they were not able to handle the situation. Jesus, on the other hand, was asleep in the rear of the boat, and they ran to Him, furious that He seemed not to care that loss of life was a real threat. Perhaps we should at least credit them with knowing where to run.

After Christ had pressed peace into the storm, He asked the

question that was central to all of their personal growth and development as spiritual leaders: "Where is your faith?" He could have asked in language I have been using, "Why isn't the bridge of your private world in better order?"

Why is it that for so many the answer to personal tension and pressure lies not in going to the bridge of life but rather in attempting to run faster, protest more vigorously, accumulate more, collect more data, and gain more expertise? We are of an age in which it seems instinctive to give attention to every cubic inch of life *other than* our inner worlds—the only place from which we can gain the strength to be brave, or even beat, any outer turbulence.

Biblical writers believed in the principle of going to the bridge; they knew and taught that the development and maintenance of our inner worlds should be our highest priority. That is one practical reason that their work has transcended all times and cultures. For what they wrote they received from the Creator *who made us to work most effectively from the inner world toward the outer.* Stephen Covey, in his book *The 7 Habits of Highly Effective People,* calls it "the inside-out approach."

One writer of Proverbs put the principle of the inner world in these words: "Watch over your heart with all diligence, / for from it flow the springs of life" (Prov. 4:23).

In one simple sentence the writer has conveyed to us a most amazing insight. What I call the "bridge," he calls the "heart." His metaphor for the heart is a spring, and suggests that out of it can flow the energy, the insight, and the force that do not succumb to outer turbulence but rather overcome it. Guard the heart, he says, and it will become a wellspring of life from which you and others can drink.

But what does it mean to "guard" the heart? For one thing, the writer is obviously concerned that the heart be protected from influences outside itself that might jeopardize its integrity. The writer is also focused on the strength and development of the heart in order to increase its capacity to bring order to one's life.

But the writer's thinking goes beyond these two ideas. He wants the reader to understand that keeping or guarding the heart, this thing I've referred to as the "bridge" in the human experience, *is a deliberate and disciplined choice a man or woman must make.* Am I being heard? We must *choose* to keep the heart. Choose! Its health and productivity cannot be assumed; it must be constantly protected and maintained.

Again, we need to remember what the captain of the submarine did when he felt something out of the ordinary going on: he immediately headed for the bridge. Why? Because he knew that that was the place in which all capability to face danger would be found. He could have commanded the spiffiest submarine in the U.S. Navy in terms of its exterior paint job, its capability for speed, and the congeniality of its crew. But if the bridge was in a state of disorder, all the rest—the paint job, the capacity for speed, and the nice guys on board—would have been meaningless.

In the New Testament, Paul made the same sort of observation when he challenged Christ-followers to "not be conformed to this [outer] world, but be transformed by the renewing of your mind" (Rom. 12:2). He's talking heart here. I've always preferred J. B. Phillip's version of this verse: "Don't let the world around you squeeze you into its own mold."

The great apostle set forth an ageless truth when he wrote this. He was directing his readers to make a right choice. Are we going to order our inner worlds, our hearts, so that they will radiate influence into the outer world? Or will we neglect our private worlds and, thus, permit the outer influences to shape us? This is a choice we must make every day of our lives.

This is an incredible thought, and it defines a core biblical issue. It is the sort of insight that the terminated executive in the

Wall Street Journal article had ignored. The evidence? His cave-in, when the world about him faced him with crushing pressure. He had no resource of inner strength from which to draw, no order to his private world.

A great name in modern missionary biography is Mary Slessor. Slessor was a young single woman who left Scotland at the turn of the twentieth century to go to a part of Africa that was then infested with disease and indescribable danger. The woman had an indomitable spirit and kept going when lesser men and women, living under the crushing pressures, broke down, ran, and never came back. Once, after a particularly draining day, she found herself trying to sleep in a crude jungle hut. Of that night she wrote:

> I am not very particular about my bed these days, but as I lay on a few dirty sticks laid across and covered with a litter of dirty corn-shells, with plenty of rats and insects, three women and an infant three days old alongside, and over a dozen sheep and goats and cows outside, you don't wonder that I slept little. *But I had such a comfortable quiet night in my own heart.*[2]

Now that is the sort of thing we are thinking about when we address the question of order in our private worlds. Whether you call it the "bridge" in naval language or the "heart" in biblical language, the point is the same: *there must be a quiet place where all is in order, a place from which comes the energy that overcomes turbulence and is not intimidated by it.*

Although he wasn't trying to make a uniquely Christian point, I nevertheless find the words of Ralph Waldo Emerson quite provocative. "It is easy in the world," he wrote, "to live after the world's opinion; it is easy in solitude to live after our own; but the great man is he who in the midst of the crowd keeps with perfect sweetness the independence of solitude."[3]

Emerson is talking heart language here.

We will know that we have learned this significant principle when we come to the point at which the development and maintenance of a strong inner world becomes the most important single function of our existence. Then in the moment when pressure rises and tension increases, we can look within and ask, "Is everything all right?" And discovering that it is, we can say, "It looks all right to me too."

THREE

CAUGHT IN A GOLDEN CAGE

IN MY EARLIER YEARS AS AN ORGANIZATIONAL LEADER, I FAILED TO appreciate the work done by a board of directors or church elders. My default perspective was that a board was like an obstacle course for a leader: board members were there to make life tough for me, and I was there to convince them that every idea I ever had was correct and richly deserved their approval.

Agree with that piece of organizational ignorance, and you are not likely to enjoy a full life of leadership. Then one night in a single meeting I learned something about myself and the organization I worked for.

Our church's elder board gathered to hear me give a final presentation on a major ministry initiative our staff wanted to launch. The board's approval would mean an increased budget, a new staff member or two, and a priority shift in our church's mission.

For an hour or more, I outlined the proposal using handouts, charts, and scribbles on a whiteboard. I turned on all my charm, probably investing all the precious influence-capital I had. When I was finished, there were questions. Lots of them. Too many questions, in fact. Some questions made me feel defensive and eroded my self-confidence. Some questions I interpreted as hostile. Where were the questions that would help support my case?

Then the time came for a vote on my proposal, and the board voted no. Can you imagine that? The board voted no! To *my* proposal. Voted no. To me. Then they turned to other business.

I was angry. I'd lost. I felt rejected. I was ready to go home and start packing my bags.

Without thinking what it looked like to others, I slid my chair back from the table and stared at the floor, never looking up. For the rest of the evening I remained silent and uninvolved, and when the chairman called the meeting to a conclusion, I tried to be the first person out the door. I would have been successful if it had not been for a man who would become one of my very dearest friends in years to come.

Al reached the door before I did. Because he was considerably larger than I was, he easily pushed me into a corner where no one could hear what he was about to say to me.

"Your performance in this meeting tonight was not very classy," Al said. "You took your shot, and you missed. They said no to you. I, for one, think you deserved that no. You didn't do your homework, and they knew it.

"Now," Al went on, "if you want them to approve everything your heart desires, then fine. But you'll have to live with the consequences all by yourself if something doesn't work. You'll save yourself a lot of grief if you realize that this board is here to help you be successful. And that means sometimes saying no to you."

What Al said to me that night is what every person who has a smidgen of "drivenness" in him or her needs to hear. He was insightful (and brave) enough to shoot a rebuke in my direction that would affect me for the rest of my leadership life. Al was telling me that I had to learn to appreciate no's, to feel grateful when better minds than mine told me the truth.

Al saved me from the need to win: from the mentality that concludes getting your way is more important than good decisions or, better yet, knowing God's purposes.

Many driven people do very good things. Driven people are not necessarily bad folk, although the consequences of their drivenness may produce unfortunate results. In fact, driven people often make great contributions. They start organizations; they provide jobs and opportunities; they are often very bright and offer ways and means of doing things that benefit many other people. Nevertheless, they are driven, and one worries about their ability to sustain the pace without danger to themselves.

I went home realizing that night that I had enough drivenness to turn me into a toxic leader. In the days and weeks to come I did a lot of homework on the symptoms of drivenness that I'd seen in others and, sadly, in myself.

Here's what I learned.

1. A DRIVEN PERSON IS GRATIFIED (AND GRATIFIED TEMPORARILY) ONLY BY ACCOMPLISHMENT. "Look at everything I'm doing. I must be special. Don't you get it? I'm special!" Somewhere in the process of maturation a driven person concludes that the only way he can feel good about himself and his world is to create a formidable list of achievements. This discovery may be the result of formative influences at an early age; as a child, affirmation and approval may have been received from a parent or influential mentor only when something had been finished. Nothing of value may have ever been said until that task was completed. Thus, the only way he could find love and acceptance was through accomplishment.

Unfortunately, when one is in a state of drivenness, the list of accomplishments never gets long enough. It must get longer and longer, more and more impressive. "Surely," the driven person reasons, "people [including my father] will like me when they see how much I can get done."

I was standing at the entrance of the arena where our grand-daughter played indoor soccer. A small boy, no older than nine, came out the door and spied his father. "I scored a goal, Dad," he said with excitement. "Yeah," his father replied, "but you missed the chance for two others."

This exchange caused me to wonder if I wasn't watching a boy who was being shaped by his father to define life and human value only in terms of accomplishment. You got one, but *you could have done more.* In such ways, a lasting message is implanted in the boy's soul, and it is done by an important authority figure.

A psychology of achievement sometimes captures the heart in circumstances like that. A person begins to reason that if one accomplishment resulted in good feelings and the praise of others, then several more accomplishments may bring an abundance of good feelings and affirmations. Or if one accomplishment (in this case, a goal) is not good enough, then perhaps three more will gain what he needs most: approval.

The driven person then begins to look for ways to accumu-late more and more achievements. He will soon be found doing two or three things at one time because that brings even more of this strange sort of pleasure. He becomes the sort of person who is always reading books and attending seminars that promise to help him use what time he has even more effectively. Why? So he can produce more accomplishments, which in turn will provide greater gratification.

This is the kind of person who sees life only in terms of results. As such, he has little appreciation for the *process* leading toward results.

2. A DRIVEN PERSON IS QUICK TO FLAUNT THE SYMBOLS OF ACCOMPLISHMENT. Titles, academic degrees, the size of a home, a corner office, a so-called trophy spouse, an invitation to an exec-utive suite at the Super Bowl, a famous name to drop: all of these

are the tools of a driven person. They arouse the envy and admiration of others. There is generally a concern for one's own notoriety. *Who,* the driven person wonders, *knows about what I am doing? How can I be better connected with the "greats" of my world?* These questions often preoccupy the driven person.

3. A DRIVEN PERSON IS USUALLY CAUGHT IN THE UNCONTROLLED PURSUIT OF EXPANSION. Driven people like to be a part of something that is always getting bigger and more successful. They are usually on the move, seeking the biggest and the best opportunities. They rarely have any time to appreciate the achievements to date.

4. DRIVEN PEOPLE TEND TO HAVE A LIMITED REGARD FOR INTEGRITY. They can become so preoccupied with the need for success and achievement that they have little time to stop and ask if their inner person is keeping pace with the outer process. Usually it is not, and there is an increasing gap, a breakdown in what Stephen Covey once called the principle-centered life.[1] People like this often become progressively deceitful; and they not only deceive others, but they also deceive themselves. In the attempt to push ahead relentlessly, they lie to themselves about motives; values and morals are compromised. Shortcuts to success become a way of life. Because the goal is so important, they drift into ethical shabbiness. Driven people become frighteningly pragmatic.

5. DRIVEN PEOPLE ARE NOT LIKELY TO ABOUND IN PEOPLE SKILLS UNLESS IT'S THE ABILITY TO MANIPULATE OR INTIMIDATE. They are not noted for creating environments in which it is a pleasure for others to work. The truth is that programs, projects, and tasks are more important to them than people. Because their eyes are on goals and objectives, they are rarely sensitive to the people about them, except as they can be used for the fulfillment of one of the goals. And if others are not found to be useful, then

they may be seen as obstacles or competitors when it comes to getting something done.

There is usually a "trail of bodies" in the wake of the driven person. Where once others praised him for his seemingly great leadership, there soon appears a steady increase in frustration and hostility as they see that the driven person cares very little about the health and growth of human beings. It becomes apparent that there is a non-negotiable agenda, and it is supreme above all other things. Colleagues and subordinates in the orbit of the driven person slowly drop away, one after another, exhausted, exploited, and disillusioned. Of this person we are most likely to find ourselves saying, "He is miserable to work with, but he certainly gets things done."

And therein lies the rub. The driven person gets things done, but he may destroy the people around him in the process. Not an attractive sight. Yet the ironic thing, which cannot be ignored, is that in almost every great organization, religious and secular, people of this sort can be found in key positions. Even though they carry with them the seeds of relational disaster, they often are indispensable to the action.

I have often recounted a moment in the lobby of our church when I was in conversation with one of our staff pastors. A woman, Marilyn, walked through the front entrance. Marilyn struggled with mental illness and was usually highly medicated. In her somewhat dazed state she often seemed a drain on people because she talked slowly and raised topics that were unimportant to busy people . . . like me (I am ashamed to admit).

Seeing Marilyn, I called out, "Hello, Marilyn. How are you?" and then quickly returned to the conversation with my colleague in the hope that she would realize I was busy and not intrude.

But that was not to be. Suddenly I was aware that Marilyn was approaching, in fact, inserting herself between me and my conversation partner. Looking up at me—she was a very short woman—she said in her slow, medicated, and monotone voice, "Pastor Mac, you say, 'Hello, Marilyn. How are you?' but you really do not want to know. You are too busy to pay attention to someone like me. I know what you think; I'm just not important enough."

Marilyn had nailed me! She had spotted drivenness in me. She knew that, in my eyes, she wasn't important enough to sustain my recognition. Perhaps many other people felt the same way but didn't have the courage to say what Marilyn said. Her medications suspended those social "inhibitors" that keep us from saying what we are thinking. She was free enough to speak her heart. I could only apologize to her and ponder the evidence that I suffered from a drivenness that caused me that day to wound a daughter of the Lord.

6. DRIVEN PEOPLE TEND TO BE HIGHLY COMPETITIVE. THEY SEE EACH EFFORT AS A WIN-OR-LOSE SITUATION. The driven person feels he must win, must look good before others, must always appear better. The more driven he is, the larger the score by which he needs to win. Winning provides the evidence the driven person desperately needs that he is right, valuable, and important. Thus, he is likely to see others as competitors or as enemies who must be beaten—perhaps even humiliated—in the process.

A man comes to mind with whom I played board games from time to time when I was a boy. It was not only important to him that he win but that he win big, as they say. If we played Monopoly, he would bankrupt me and then (stretching the rules) insist on "loaning" me money to keep me playing on so that he could win a second time. If we were playing Scrabble, he would run up the score with his far superior vocabulary and keep me struggling in the game even though I had lost heart and interest a long time before. To this day, board games are something I will do anything to avoid (much to my family's chagrin). The echoes of the repeated humiliations years ago remain with me. Driven people do this to others.

7. A DRIVEN PERSON OFTEN POSSESSES A VOLCANIC FORCE OF ANGER, WHICH CAN ERUPT ANYTIME HE OR SHE SENSES OPPOSITION OR DISLOYALTY. This anger can be triggered when people disagree, offer an alternative solution to a problem, or even hint at just a bit of criticism.

The anger may not surface as physical violence. But it can take the form of verbal brutality: profanity or humiliating insults, for example. The anger can express itself in vindictive acts such as firing people, slandering them before peers, or simply denying them things they have come to expect, such as affection, money, or even companionship.

Frankly, I would not have believed the story had it not been told by a person I trust. Picture an open office of a small business with several working associates. The office manager, a woman who has worked in the office for fifteen years, has made a request to the business owner for a week off to be with a sick baby. When he refuses, she responds tearfully, asking him to reconsider. Big mistake! When he sees her tears, he snarls, "Clean out your desk and get out of here; I don't need you anyhow." When she is gone, he turns to the horrified onlookers and says, "Let's get one thing straight; you're all here for only one reason: to make money for this business. And if you don't like that, get out right now!"

Tragically, many good people who surround the driven person are more than willing to absorb the impact of such anger, although it desperately hurts them, because they reason that the boss or the leader is good at what he or she does. Sometimes the anger and its cruel effects are accepted simply because no one has either the courage or the ability to stand up to the driven person.

A person who served on the board of a major Christian organization once told me of encounters with the executive director that included outbursts of rage studded with extraordinary profanity and abusive language. When I asked why board members accepted such behavior, which was neither rare nor excusable, he said, "I guess we've been so impressed with the way God seems to use him in his public presentations that we are reluctant to confront him. I guess we don't think we can afford to lose him."

8. DRIVEN PEOPLE BOAST OF THEIR BUSYNESS. THEY HAVE FORGOTTEN HOW TO PLAY. SPIRITUAL ACTIVITY SEEMS A WASTE OF TIME. They are usually too busy for the pursuit of ordinary relationships in marriage, family, or friendship, or even to carry on a relationship with themselves—not to speak of one with God. Because driven people rarely think they have accomplished enough, they seize every available minute to attend more meetings, to study more material, to initiate more projects. They operate on the precept that a reputation for busyness is a sign of success and personal importance. Thus, they attempt to impress people with the fullness of their schedules. They may even express a high level of self-pity, bemoaning the "trap" of responsibility they claim to be in, wishing aloud that there was some possible release from all that they have to live with. But just try to suggest a way out!

The truth is that the very worst thing that could happen to them would be if someone provided them with a way out. They wouldn't know what to do with themselves if there were suddenly less to do. Busyness for the driven person becomes a habit, a way of life and thought. They find it enjoyable to complain and gather pity, and they would probably not want it any different. But tell a driven person that, and you'll make him or her angry.

This then is the driven person—not an entirely attractive picture. What often disturbs me as I look at this picture is the fact that much of our world is run by driven people. We have created a system that rides on their backs. And where that is true in businesses, in churches, and in homes, the growth of people is often sacrificed for accomplishment and accumulation.

Pastors who are driven men or women have been known to

burn out scores of assistants and lay leaders because of their need to head organizations that are the biggest, the best, and the most well known. There are businesspeople who claim Christian faith and who have enjoyed a reputation for graciousness in the church, but who are ruthless in the office, pushing people and squeezing them for the last ounce of energy simply so they themselves can enjoy the gratification of winning, accumulating, or establishing a reputation.

Among the more painful self-revelations of my life was that I am basically a driven person. I have, at one time or another, seen in myself almost all the traits I have listed. That drivenness has created moments of crisis for me down through the years. And each time I had to come to grips with fresh new revelations of an insidious energy within me that wanted to achieve and accomplish things for reasons that were far from obedience to Jesus or the glory of God.

What I had to learn was that my drivenness needed to be consecrated on a daily basis. I had to listen to my wife and to those closest to me to see if they saw any of the signs of uncontrolled drivenness. I had to engage in regular self-examination to ensure that the plans I was making, the leadership I was giving, the goals I was setting were more in alignment with "calledness" than drivenness. I had to learn how to listen to God and ensure that I was moving according to His agenda and not my self-serving one. To ignore the possibility that my life could be taken over by the spirit of drivenness would be to my peril.

Some time ago a businessman became a Christ-follower through the witness of a layman who is a good friend of mine. Not long after making his choice to follow Jesus Christ, he wrote a long letter to my friend who had guided him into faith. In it he described some of his struggles as the result of his driven condition. I requested permission to share part of the letter because it so vividly illustrated the driven person. He wrote:

Several years ago I was at a point of great frustration in my life. Although I had a wonderful wife and three beautiful sons, my career was going badly. I had few friends, my oldest son began getting into trouble—he started failing in school—I was suffering from depression, there was great tension and unhappiness in my family. At that time I had an opportunity to travel overseas where I stayed to work in a foreign company. This new opportunity was such an excellent one, financially and career-wise, that I made it number one in my life, forsaking all other values. I did many wrong (i.e., sinful) things to advance my position and success. I justified them as being of good consequence to my family (more money, etc.), which resulted in my lying to myself and my family and behaving wrongly in many ways.

Of course, this was intolerable to my wife, and she and my family returned to the U.S. I was still blind, however, to the problems that were within me. My success, my salary, my career—all moved upward. I was *caught in a golden cage*.

Although many wonderful things were happening outside me, inside I was losing everything. My capacity to reason and my capacity to decide were both weakened. I would evaluate alternatives, constantly going over various options, always trying to pick the one that would maximize success and career. I knew in my heart that something was terribly wrong. I went to church, but the words there couldn't reach me. I was too caught up in my own world.

After a terrible episode with my family several weeks ago, I completely gave up my course of thinking and went to a hotel room for nine days to figure out what to do. The more I thought, the more troubled I became. I began to realize how dead I really was, how so much of my life was dark. And worse than that, I could see no way out. My only solution was to run and hide, to start in a different place, to sever all connections.

This brutal description of a man at the bottom fortunately has a happy ending. For not long after his nine-day experience in a hotel room, he discovered the love of God and its capacity to engender dramatic change in his life. And a driven man turned into—what I say in a future chapter—a *called* man. He got out of his "golden cage."

In the Bible, few men typify the driven man better than Saul, the first king of Israel. Unlike the previous story, which had a happy conclusion, this one has a miserable ending, for Saul never got out of his golden cage. All he did was heap increasing amounts of stress upon himself. And it destroyed him.

The Bible's introduction to Saul should be warning enough that the man had some flaws that, if not addressed within his inner world, would cause him quickly to lose personal control.

> There was a man of Benjamin whose name was Kish the son of Abiel, the son of Zeror, the son of Becorath, the son of Aphiah, the son of a Benjamite, a mighty man of valor. He had a son whose name was Saul, a choice and handsome man, and there was not a more handsome person than he among the sons of Israel; from his shoulders and up he was taller than any of the people. (1 Sam. 9:1–2)

Saul possessed three unearned characteristics at the beginning of his public life that had the potential to become assets or serious liabilities. Which they would be was his choice. And how Saul made those choices depended on the daily order of his private world.

The three characteristics? First, wealth; second, an attractive appearance; and third, a physically large and well-developed body. All were attributes of a person's public world. In other words, the initial impression was that Saul was a better man than anyone around him. All three external marks commanded attention and gained him quick advantages. (Each time I think of Saul's natural gifts, I recall the bank president who said to me some years ago, "MacDonald, you could go a long way in the business world if you were about six inches taller.") And, most important, they provided Saul with a sort of charisma that made possible his achieving some early success without ever having to develop a heart of wisdom or spiritual stature. He was simply a fast starter.

As Saul's story unfolds in the biblical text, we learn some other things about the man, things that could have either contributed to his success or become a part of his ultimate failure. We are told, for example, that he was good with words. When he was given a chance to speak before crowds, he was eloquent. The stage was set for a man to consolidate power and command recognition without ever having to develop any sense of a strong inner world first. And that was where the danger lay.

When Saul became king of Israel, he enjoyed too much immediate success. It apparently made him unaware that he had any limits to his life. He spent little time pondering his need for others, engendering a relationship with God, or even facing his responsibilities toward the people over whom he ruled. The signs of a driven man began to appear.

Saul became a busy man; he saw worlds he thought needed conquering. Thus, when he faced an impending battle with the Philistines, Israel's great enemy of the day, and waited at Gilgal for Samuel the prophet to come and offer the necessary sacrifices, he grew impatient and irritable when the holy man did not arrive on time. Saul felt that his timetable was being compromised; he had to get on with things. His remedy? Offer the sacrifice himself. And that is exactly what he did.

The result? A rather serious breach of covenant with God. Offering sacrifice was the kind of thing prophets like Samuel did, not kings like Saul. But Saul had forgotten that because he saw himself as being too important.

From that time forward Saul found himself on a downhill track. "Now your kingdom shall not endure. The LORD has sought out for Himself a man after His own heart" (1 Sam. 13:14). This is how most driven men end.

Stripped of what blessing and assistance he had had from God up to this point, Saul's drivenness began to reveal itself even further. Soon all of his energies became consumed in holding on to his throne, competing with young David, who had caught the imagination of the people of Israel.

The Scriptures give several examples of Saul's explosive anger, which drove him to outrage as well as to moments of paralyzing self-pity. By the end of his life, he was a man out of control, seeing enemies behind every bush. Why? Because from the very beginning Saul had been a driven man, and he had never cultivated the order of his private world.

Saul never came to grips with his drivenness. He would not have lasted long among the twelve disciples Jesus picked because his own compulsions were far too strong. That which had driven him to grasp power and not let go, that which had caused him to turn on his closest supporters, and that which caused him to make a successive series of unwise decisions, finally led him to a humiliating death. He was the classic driven man.

To the extent that we see him in ourselves, we have work to do in our private worlds. For an inner life fraught with unresolved drives will not be able to hear clearly the voice of Christ when He calls. The noise and pain of stress will be too great.

Unfortunately, our society abounds with Sauls, men and women caught in golden cages, driven to accumulate, to be recognized, or to achieve. Our churches, unfortunately, abound with these driven people as well. Many churches are fountains gone dry. Rather than being springs of life-giving energy that cause people to grow and to delight in God's way, they become sources of stress. The driven man's private world is disordered. His cage may be lavishly golden, but it's a trap; inside there is nothing that lasts.

FOUR

THE TRAGIC TALE OF A SUCCESSFUL LOSER

ON A TABLE IN THE ROOM WHERE I DO MY WRITING IS A SIZEABLE model of a nineteenth-century sailboat that seamen call a schooner.

The boat, carved by a Polish sailor from a solid block of wood, was given to me almost forty years ago.

The man who gave me the boat had asked to talk with me about his broken life. His health was bad; his family was angry with him; he had no friends; he couldn't identify anything that he did for fun.

Why would he seek me out?

He'd read something I'd written, thought I might have some secret that could help him, and, on impulse, called me on the phone.

We had several conversations over a period of weeks. After one of them he mentioned a model boat in his home and suggested that it might add a "New Englandish" flavor to my office décor.

Although I am not a boat person, I must have indicated interest because he brought the boat with him the next time we met. I liked it, and it has been mine ever since. (I had a dream one night that I brought the boat to one of those antique shows on television, and the expert on model boats said that my boat had been owned by a Russian czar and was worth $540,000.)

Since the boat occupies a prominent place in my office, there are few days when I do not glance in its direction and wonder what happened to the man who made it a gift to me. We lost touch many years ago.

So why was his life falling apart? It became apparent during our conversations that the man was addicted to his work. The business he owned was his religion, his mistress, his reason for being.

I remember pulling from him the details of his workaholic lifestyle. Ten to twelve hours a day, seven days a week at his office. When he reached home (often late in the evening), he would deal with customers on the phone as he wolfed down a cold supper. If there was any time to watch a bit of television, he multitasked by glancing occasionally at the screen while he fingered through spreadsheets from his briefcase. (Laptops were not yet in vogue.)

There were no vacations, no romantic weekends with his wife at an inn in Vermont, no male friendships, and certainly no church or community life.

A most revealing moment in our conversations came when I asked why a man would want to live as he was living. How had his work become such an idol?

"Work has always been an idol," he confessed. "It's the only thing I ever did that caused my father to be pleased with me. And even that wasn't very often."

"Your father," I said. "What was he like?"

"I despised him," he responded. "Still do."

When I asked about such strong feelings, he said something like this: "My father believed that the only thing worth doing in life was to work. He avoided my mother; he had no friends. Vacations, playing, hobbies were a waste of time to him. So what's left? Your work!

"So that's the way he raised me: to work just as much and just as well as he thought he worked. He was almost never satisfied with anything I did. If I heard it once, I heard it a thousand times.

He'd look at something I'd just finished—clean out the garage, wash the car, mow the lawn—and then he'd point out the places where I'd screwed up. 'You know, kid,' he'd say, 'you're a loser, and you'll always be a loser.'

"You won't believe that I hear those words every day of my life . . . even though the bastard's been dead for years. 'You know, kid, you're a loser, and you'll always be a loser.'"

Time to interrupt him.

"So let me tell you what I'm hearing," I said. "If you're ever tempted to shut down the office early—if you feel the urge to go to a Red Sox game, if you dare to sit down to eat dinner or watch TV, if you think you ought to be at your kid's soccer game or take your wife out on a date, you start hearing your father shouting in the back of your head saying, 'No, no, no—you're a loser'?"

"Yeah, precisely. "You've got it! That's what I hear."

Instead, he wanted to hear his father finally say, "Son, you're not a loser; I was really, really wrong."

What made this matter more bizarre was that the unpleasable father had been dead for *several* years. Yet the son, now in midlife, continued to work to gain an imagined approval. What had started as an objective became a habit of living, an addiction, you could say, which he could not break.

Many of us with these kinds of stories spend a lifetime trying to prove our accusers wrong. We keep trying harder and harder and harder, hoping that one day a father or a mother or some voice we care about will say to us, "You know, I've never told you this, but I've always been terribly proud of all you've accomplished. I probably pushed you too hard. I'm sorry about that."

I've been a part of more than a few conversations where someone offers a version of this story. And I'm sensitive to each storyteller because I grew up in a home where my father was similarly unpleasable. I used to hear the equivalent of that father's words myself.

For a short time in my early adult years, I experienced several periods of migraine-type headaches. I was referred to a doctor who specialized in this kind of thing. He examined me and then invited me to his office.

"I've treated a lot of men, fewer women, with headaches like yours," he told me. "They come to me thinking all they need is some kind of painkiller, and they are disappointed when I tell them I can't put them on such strong drugs for an extended period of time."

When I asked what I was supposed to do, he said, "Well, I could be wrong, but I'm thinking that you've had some difficulties with someone, like your father . . . or maybe your mother . . . or somebody else of significance in the past. They may have told you that you weren't measuring up, that you had to do better at this or that. So you developed the habit of trying to earn their approval. Here's the thing: because you're not getting what you want, you're probably carrying a lot of anger deep inside of you. Anger and headaches tend to go together in more than a few people. Maybe you're one of them. Possible?"

I'd never thought about this kind of thing before.

"Here's the bad news," he said. "You're not likely to ever get that approval. Especially if whoever this is has already died. If they're still alive, the chances are that they'll *never* give you want you're wanting. So forget it. It's not going to come.

"So I've got a better idea," he went on. "Why don't you simply work on forgiving whoever it is that is failing you in this area? Get beyond this. That's most likely the best answer to your headache problem. Less expensive too."

When I returned home, Gail asked what the doctor said.

"He says I have to forgive my father."

"Do we have to pay for that advice?" Gail asked. I said I thought we would have to.

In the months that followed that conversation with the doctor,

I tried to observe myself carefully. I concluded that the doctor might be on to something. I came to see how often a part of me imagined my father standing off to one side and telling me how delighted he was with the things I accomplished. And I realized that the doctor was correct when he said this would probably never happen. How could my father be delighted with me *when he wasn't delighted with himself?*

One day I recalled Eric Liddel's words to his sister in the movie *Chariots of Fire*: "When I run, I feel God's pleasure." Those were the words that described what I was seeking and what the man who had given me the model boat had so badly wanted. Our fathers' pleasure.

It was from that insight that the word *driven* came to mean something to me. I was a man *driven* to gain the pleasure of my father, and it didn't stop there. It became the basis for my need to gain the approval of *anyone* who was in an authoritative position with me: bosses, board members, powerful people, successful people, demanding people.

I began what I can only call a daily liturgy of forgiveness. Each morning I would kneel and pray. Somehow I thought the kneeling process would add sincerity to what I was trying to do. In these moments, I would imagine myself approaching Jesus in the company of my father. I would declare to Jesus that, for another day, I was choosing to renounce my resentment toward my father, that I wished for our relationship to become peaceable.

Looking back at what I did, I realize that the secret was that forgiving my father had to be a daily experience. Sometimes even more than daily. A one-time "Okay, Dad, I forgive you" would never have been sufficient. I had to forgive and re-forgive my father day after day for at least six months. And occasionally, since then, I have had to repeat the process.

Here's the part that will have a few people struggling with the credulity of this story. *I never, ever had another headache.*

I want to make it very clear that I am not describing my experience with a mind that everyone else should do the same thing. This is my story. This was the way heaven chose to deal with me.

The important piece here is to take note of the habit pattern of drivenness. Drivenness is similar to an addiction that needs a much longer-range perspective.

Once sensitized to the notion of drivenness, I began to see it not only in myself but in many, many others around me. I began to wonder if the top echelon of people in any walk of life (professionals, scholars, athletes, politicians, business people, and, yes, even religious leaders) are probably *driven* people, driven to do noble things (most of the time) but often for less-than-best reasons. Like me.

WHY ARE PEOPLE DRIVEN?

Why do so many people appear to be driven? My friend, who had given me the boat, is an extreme example of one reason. He typifies those who grew up in *environments where "well done" was never heard.* When such acceptance and affirmation is lacking, it is by no means unusual for the respect-starved person to conclude that more work, greater accumulation of symbols of success, or worldly praise will finally convince some significant person (a parent, for example) who has withheld approval to finally say, "Son (Daughter), you are not a loser after all. I'm terribly proud to be your father."

Many people in leadership positions share this sort of background and this sort of insecurity. Some leaders appear to be highly benevolent people, doing good things, and are praised for dedicated, selfless actions; the fact may be that they are pushed toward the hope of gaining the acceptance and approval of just one significant person in their past. And if they cannot gain that, then they develop an insatiable appetite for applause, wealth, or power from other sources, attempting to compensate for the loss. Rarely, however, is satisfaction reached. This is because their pursuit is in the public world; the private world is left empty and wanting. And that is where the real ache lies.

Another source of drivenness is an early experience of serious deprivation or shame. In his book *Creative Suffering*, Paul Tournier points out that an enormous number of world political leaders over the past several centuries have been orphans. Having grown up in a context of personal loss in terms of intimate parental love and emotional closeness, they may have sought a compensatory experience in the embrace of the crowds. Behind their great drive for power may be the simple need for love. Rather than meeting this need through the ordering of the private world within, they have chosen to pursue it on the external level.[1]

Driven people can also come from backgrounds in which there has been a sense of great shame or embarrassment. My library includes a remarkably candid book: *The Man Who Could Do No Wrong* by Charles Blair. In it he described his own childhood during the Depression days in Oklahoma. With pain he recalled his daily task of hauling the free government-issue milk from the local firehouse to home. As he carried the milk pail down the street, he had to endure what he felt was raw scorn from boys his own age. Out of the agony of such moments came the resolve that the day would come when he would never again carry a symbolic milk pail, which signified a feeling of worthlessness.

Blair tells the story of an unforgettable walk home from school in the company of a girl for whom he had strong feelings. Suddenly a boy with a shiny new bicycle came up beside them and offered the girl a ride. Without hesitation she hopped on to the back fender, leaving Blair behind as she and the other boy rode off together. The humiliation of that moment caused Blair to quietly resolve that someday he would have the equivalent of a shiny bicycle, that he would have the wherewithal to make impressions that would command the attentions and loyalties of others.

And those resolves burned their way into his life. They became a source of the drive that subsequently, by his own account, betrayed him. He would later need to own the most attractive automobile, lead the most beautiful and largest church, and wear the most stylish of men's fashions. These things would prove that he had made it out of the Oklahoma Depression. He was not worthless; he was not poor. He could prove it. Look!

Charles Blair was running from something, and that meant that he had to run toward something. Although his drive was clothed in all sorts of impressive spiritual motives, and although his ministry was remarkably effective, down at the center were unresolved hurts of the past. Because these hurts remained a point of disorder in his private world, they came back to haunt him. They affected his choices and values and blinded him to what was happening at a crucial moment of his life. The result? Serious disaster. Failure, embarrassment, and public humiliation.

But it must be added that he rebounded. That alone suggests hope for the driven man or woman. Charles Blair, the *driven* man of earlier years, running from shame, was now a *called* man, and he deserved the admiration of his friends. I consider his book to be one of the most significant I have ever read. It ought to be required reading for any man or woman who is in leadership.

Finally, *some people are simply raised in an environment where drivenness is a way of life.* In *Wealth Addiction*, Philip Slater details the backgrounds of several living billionaires. In almost every account there is indication that as children, these billionaires made the accumulation of things and the conquest of people their amusement. There was little if any play for the purpose of pure fun or exercise. They only knew how to win, how to accumulate. It was what they saw their parents doing, and they assumed that it was the only way to live. Thus, the drive to grow rich and powerful began in the earliest days.

To such people an ordered private world has little meaning. The only thing worth giving attention to is the public world, where things can be measured, admired, and used.

Of course, driven people come out of many other backgrounds, and these are but a few samples. But one thing is sure in all cases: driven people will never enjoy the tranquility of an ordered private world. Their prime targets are all external, material, and measurable. Nothing else seems real; nothing else makes much sense. And it all must be held on to, as it was with Saul, who found that power was more important than the integrity of a friendship with David.

Let us be sure we understand that when we speak of driven people, we are not merely thinking of a highly competitive businessperson or a professional athlete. We are considering something much more pervasive than workaholism. Any of us can look within and suddenly discover that *drivenness is our way of life*. We can be driven toward a superior Christian reputation, toward a desire for some dramatic spiritual experience, or toward a form of leadership that is more of a quest for domination of people than servanthood. A homemaker can be a driven person, and so can a student. A driven person can be any of us.

HOPE FOR THE DRIVEN PERSON

Can the driven person be changed? Most certainly. It begins when such a person faces up to the fact that he or she is operating according to drives and not calls. That discovery is usually made in the blinding, searching light of an encounter with Christ. As the twelve disciples discovered, an audience with Jesus over a period of time exposes all the roots and expressions of drivenness.

To deal with drivenness, one must begin to ruthlessly appraise one's own motives and values, just as Peter was forced to do in his periodic confrontations with Jesus. The person seeking relief from drivenness will find it wise to listen to mentors and critics who speak Christ's words to us today.

The driven person may have some humbling acts of renunciation, some disciplined gestures of surrender of things—not necessarily bad things but things that have been important for all the wrong reasons. Perhaps he will have to grant forgiveness to some of those who in the past never offered the proper kind of affection and affirmation. And all of that may be just the beginning.

Paul the apostle in his pre-Christian days was driven. As a driven man, he studied, he joined, he attained, he defended, and he was applauded. The pace at which he was operating shortly before his conversion was almost manic. He was driven toward some elusive goal, and later, when he could look back at that lifestyle with all of its compulsions, he would say, "It was all worthless."

Paul was driven until Christ called him. One gets the feeling that when Paul fell to his knees before the Lord while on the road to Damascus, there was an explosion of relief within his private world. What a change from the drivenness that had pushed him toward Damascus in an attempt to stamp out Christianity to that dramatic moment when, in complete submission, he asked Jesus Christ, "What shall I do, Lord?" A driven man was converted into a called one.

I could have wished this for the man who came to talk with me about his father. Time after time we talked about his insatiable drive to win, to earn, to impress. There were a few occasions when I thought he was catching the message, when I allowed myself to be convinced we were making progress. I believed that he was going to move the center of his life from the public aspect of his world to the private side.

I could almost see him kneeling before Christ, offering up

his drivenness, being washed clean of all the old, terribly painful memories of a father who had flung the sense of being a loser into his private world. How much I wanted my friend, the successful loser, to see himself as a disciple called by Christ, and not one driven to achieve in order to prove something.

"Why don't you simply work on forgiving your father?" I asked the man who had given me the boat one more time.

"Can't," he responded. "I just can't . . . can't imagine doing it."

"So you prefer the pathway you're on. The one that's going to cost you your marriage, your children, and your future grandchildren. You prefer loneliness, heart attacks, and a deserted soul?"

"I'll think about it."

I never saw again the man who had given me the boat.

And then there's me. Although I did experience a breakthrough of forgiveness toward my father, he was never able to reciprocate. Our last years were marked by a silence that was deafening. My father never knew his grandchildren; he never was able to enjoy a family line of men and women who wanted to know God's pleasure.

Then came the last days of his life. When I asked if I could come to see him, he indicated that he would like to see me. When I came to his hospital room, it was clear that he was dying. "Who are you?" he looked up from his bed and asked.

"I'm Gordon. I'm your son," I said.

"Why are you here?" he asked.

"I've come to say one more time that there is peace between us. That I love you, and that I'm thankful that you have been my father."

His last words to me? "I'm sorry; I'm sorry; I'm sorry."

Two days later he was gone.

FIVE

LIVING AS A CALLED PERSON

IF YOU RIDE THE TRAIN FROM NEW YORK CITY TO BOSTON, YOU WILL pass through a large railroad yard where hundreds of railcars are parked until needed to transport people or freight.

When I was a boy, six or seven years old, my grandmother took me to this train yard to watch the trainmen at work. For several hours we saw how the passenger and freight cars were sorted and shuttled from track to track and then coupled together behind an enormous steam locomotive for a cross-country trip.

At one end of the rail yard, there was a large mechanical device called a round table. It was built to turn those big locomotives in different directions. More than anything else we saw that day, I remember the round table most of all. Maybe that's because of something my grandmother said about it.

"I think," she said, "God has a round table too. He uses it to change the pathway of people He's calling to serve Him. He may put you on his round table someday. You'll think you're going one way, but His round table will send you off in a different direction."

Recently, while on a Boston-bound train, I happened to be looking out the window when we passed through the railroad yard my grandmother and I had visited many years ago. I wondered if

43

the old round table was still there, and, to my delight, I saw it a moment later. But now it was rusting, falling apart from disuse.

Then I remembered my grandmother's use of the round table to plant a thought in my young head. "God has a round table too. He uses it to change the pathway of people He's *calling* to serve Him."

In my last year of graduate school, I flew back and forth across the United States speaking to groups of businesspeople about Christian discipleship. Often I spent the weekend in private homes rather than hotels.

The unanticipated blessing of that private-home hospitality was the conversations I had with men and women who spent enormous amounts of hours each week in the marketplace. Had these conversations happened on church property, I imagine we would have limited ourselves to the issues of church programs and politics.

But when I stayed in homes, I found people much more willing to talk plainly about the place of a Christ-follower in their homes and in the world of work. I heard about opportunities, discouragements, confusions, and the meaning of success.

Our conversations often led to a great question: *How do we equip ourselves to live in the steps of Jesus from Monday morning to Saturday night?*

"We love our pastor; he's a very caring man," I often heard. "But he knows little about the world in which I work. His sermons are wonderful, but they seem mostly to be about the ways we do things on church property. He has no idea how to speak to the issues I live with in the working world."

I often had free time on Monday mornings, which allowed me to visit the places where my weekend hosts worked. I met their bosses, their secretaries, their working associates. I toured the places where factory workers, salespeople, schoolteachers, and truck drivers generated their incomes. I went out to construction sites, airports, and warehouses. It was an education that my graduate school professors could never have given me.

I listened as people talked about the upsides and downsides of their work. I learned that many people hate their jobs. I heard about moral and ethical issues, boredom, fear, and serious injustices. There were exchanges about cutthroat competition for advancement, racial and gender issues, sexual harassment, and the meaning of ambition in the life of a Christ-follower.

If privacy was possible, I often left my hosts with a prayer that God would be present with them each day at work.

When I arrived home on most Monday nights, Gail was there to meet me at the airport, and our conversation in the car would quickly turn to the people I'd met and spent time with that weekend.

"If I was this person's pastor," I'd say, "I'd be out where they worked as often as possible. I'd be preaching about this, about that. I'd give anything to motivate them to think about how Jesus could be present through them in their workplace."

On one of those Mondays—in the middle of such a conversation—Gail interrupted me and said, "If you listened to yourself, you'd realize that God is telling you what He wants you to do. He's calling you to be a new kind of pastor who tries his best to help people make Christian sense out of the places where they live and work."

And that's how I heard God's call to become a pastor.

THE CALLED PERSON

Driven people—Israel's King Saul comes to mind—may not always end well, but a person who has lived in the center of God's call tells a different story.

The Bible is populated with the stories of called men and women. Somewhere along life's way each was round-tabled by God. Result: a different, unexpected direction.

The Old Testament prophet Jeremiah is an excellent example. When he first heard the call of God to be a prophet, he was resistant. "I do not know how to speak; I am too young" (Jer. 1:6 NIV).

God sped up the round table, saying, "I appoint you over nations and kingdoms to uproot and tear down, to destroy and overthrow, to build and to plant" (v. 10 NIV).

That's a call. That's a change of direction from a recessive priestly life to that of a formidable prophet who would confront kings and power brokers and become the voice of God to them.

When I reflect on the nature of called people, I turn first to those whom Jesus chose to be at His side for three years: the disciples. Few, if any of them, would have been candidates for high positions in organized religion or big business. It is not that they were unusually awkward. It is just that they appeared to be absolutely ordinary. We have to keep reminding ourselves: no headhunter in his or her right mind would have vetted most of them for leadership in the kingdom of God. But the Lord saw qualities in them that no one else detected. To each He gave the familiar call that rabbis used to invite disciples to their side: "Follow me!"

After three intense years of training, they began to morph into champions. Little by little people could see the influence of Jesus in them. The round table had turned and pointed in the direction of a new way.

The Scriptures are dotted with called men and women, of course. Mary, mother of Jesus, should be near or at the top of any list of called people. Mary seems to have been a diminutive young woman from a backwater town who was suddenly visited by an angel. Soon she was the recipient of what you'd describe as a call, a summons from God to be the mother of the Messiah, the Christ. Talk about being round-tabled.

Caleb (of Joshua and Caleb fame) sure qualifies. "I . . . followed the LORD my God wholeheartedly," he said as he summed up his life (Josh. 14:8 NIV). Or Stephen, reputed to be the first Christian martyr: "a man full of faith and of the Holy Spirit" (Acts 6:5). Great lines, these.

Abraham was called to leave his motherland and become the father of a new nation. Moses was called to affect the liberation of the Hebrews from Egyptian slavery. Isaiah was called to communicate a message that would become the core of the words of John the Baptizer, Jesus, and Paul. Nehemiah heard a call to lead in the rebuilding of Jerusalem. The list of the round-tabled—the called ones—goes on and on.

My favorite from among the called ones? I choose John the Baptizer. I must tell you that this man has been an inspiration to me during the highest and the lowest moments of my life. There's a sense in which John has always been there for me when I have needed perspective and resettling. Perhaps you can let his story wash over you as it has often washed over me.

THE MAN WHO LOST HIS JOB

Start with courage. John the Baptizer abounded in it. When the crowds from Jerusalem and Judea came streaming to the Jordan River valley to take his measure, John had the audacity to tell them that they ought to back off from exonerating themselves based on their claim to racial or religious superiority. Name your sins, he said. Express your genuine sorrow over them. Renounce your claims to racial and religious superiority. Recognize that your need for spiritual and moral renewal is as great as any other people-group in the world. Amazingly, they (most, anyway) listened.

The baptism (usually a ceremony reserved for Gentiles), he claimed, would be good for them. It would offer proof of the genuineness of their long-awaited contrition. His words must have driven the sanctimonious men in the crowd mad.

No wonder no one was ever neutral about John. The man never wasted words, never flattered a soul. You loved him or hated him. You're probably aware that one of the haters eventually removed his head. But only after John had finished his work.

Humanly speaking, John didn't have much going for him in terms of an attractive public world. We assume his parents died while he was quite young. He grew up in the desert where he partook of an austere diet and wore off-brand clothing. You can only conclude that you are watching a man with extraordinary inner strength and orientation.

John, this called man, is a marked contrast to the Old Testament's King Saul, a driven man from the start. John seems to have had from the very beginning a vivid sense of destiny, the result of a heavenly assignment that came from deep within as he immersed himself in the writings of Isaiah.

One sees the contrast between Saul and John most vividly when their personal identities and their sense of vocational security are under attack. Saul, the driven man, you will remember, reacted violently, lashing out at the younger David as he followed him all over the desert in an attempt to destroy him. And each time he encountered David, he appeared more foolish than he'd been previously.

But John is another story. Watch him when the observation is made that his popularity may be headed into serious decline. To put it another way, study John when he learns that he is losing his job.

The moment I have in mind comes after John has introduced Christ to the multitudes and they have begun to transfer
their affections to this "Lamb of God" (John 1:36). It is brought to
John's attention that the crowds, even some of his own disciples,
are turning to Jesus, listening to His teaching and being baptized
by His disciples. One gets the feeling that those who brought the
news to John concerning the decline of his ratings may have anticipated (even hoped?) that they would get the chance to see John
react just a bit negatively. But if that was the case, they were to be
disappointed.

> A man can receive nothing unless it has been given him
> from heaven. You yourselves are my witnesses that I said,
> "I am not the Christ," but "I have been sent ahead of Him."
> He who has the bride is the bridegroom; but the friend of
> the bridegroom, who stands and hears him, rejoices greatly
> because of the bridegroom's voice. So this joy of mine has
> been made full. He must increase, but I must decrease.
> (John 3:27–30)

So what is John saying here? He's teaching us what *called*
means.

Called People Understand Stewardship

First, John's comments begin with the principle of *stewardship*. Those who have instigated this conversation apparently
believe that John will be rattled when he hears that his life as a
crowd gatherer is over. But, in fact, he was anything but rattled.
He seems, rather, to have been delighted. I imagine John watching
the crowds moving away from him and toward Jesus, and he is
delighted. I hear him saying, "They were never, ever mine. They

were loaned to me by heaven." Called people *never* assume owner-ship of their work or the people of that work.

How different this is from the driven Saul, who assumed that he owned his throne in Israel and could do anything with it that he wished. When one owns something, it must be held on to; it has to be protected. But John did not think that way. So when Christ came to compel the crowds, John was only too glad to hand them off and get out of the way.

John's view of stewardship presents us with an important contemporary principle. For his crowds may be our careers, our assets, our natural and spiritual gifts, our health. So—and think before answering!—are these things owned, or merely managed in the name of the One who gave them? Driven people consider them owned; called people do not. When driven people lose those things, it is a major crisis. When called people lose them, nothing of substance changes. The private world remains the same, per-haps even stronger.

I love the words of Cardinal Danneels of Brussels:

> When I get home after a long day, I go to the chapel and pray. I say to the Lord, "There it is for today; things are finished. Now let's be serious, is this diocese mine or yours?" The Lord says, "What do you think?" I answer, "I think it's yours." "That is true," the Lord says, "it is mine." And so I say, "Listen, Lord, it is your turn to take responsibility for and direct the diocese. I'm going now to sleep."[1]

Called People Know Exactly Who They Are

A second quality of calledness is seen in John's certainty of his own identity. Let me paraphrase his remarks. You will remem-ber that he said to his visitors: "I've told you often *who I am not*: namely, the Christ." Knowing who he was not was the beginning of

50

knowing who he was. And John had no illusions as to his personal identity. That had already been established in his interior, private world. *You are John, son of Zecharias and Elizabeth. You may be a great prophet, a dazzling preacher—but you are not the Christ!*

By contrast, those whose private worlds are in disarray tend to get their identities confused. They can have an increasing inability to separate role from person. What they *do* is indistinguishable from who they *are*. That is why people who have wielded great power and enjoyed positions of privilege find it very difficult to give them up, and will often fight to the death to retain what they've had. It is why retirement is difficult for more than a few men and women. And it helps to explain why a mother may suffer depression when her last child has left the home. Come to think of it, I was the one who felt the depression when our kids left home. Apparently, it works either way.

We need to ponder this matter of identity carefully, for it happens to be a very contemporary subject. John could easily have taken advantage of the crowd's gullibility during the early days when he was popular. Or he could have been seduced by their applause. The fact that the masses were switching their favor from the priests of Jerusalem to him could have supercharged him with arrogance and ambition. It would have been rather simple to nod yes to questions as to whether he was the Messiah.

I suspect that there was a small window of time when he could have gotten away with making outlandish claims about himself. You can almost hear a man of lesser integrity than John in a moment of weakness saying, "Me, the Messiah? Well, I hadn't thought about it quite like some are saying it, but perhaps they're right, there is something kind of Messiah-like about me. Why don't I fly with this idea of Messiahship for a while and see what transpires?"

If that had been John, he probably could have pulled off the hoax for a short while. But the genuine John would not even try.

His inner sphere was too well ordered for him not to have seen through the terrible implications of a misplaced identity.

If there was a moment when the crowd's praise became thunderous, the voice of God from within John was even louder. And that voice spoke more convincingly because John had first ordered his inner world out in the desert.

Don't underestimate the significance of this principle. Today in our media-fashioned world many good and talented leaders face the constant temptation to begin believing the text of their own publicity releases. And if they do, a messianic fantasy gradually infects their personalities and leadership styles. Forgetting who they are not, they begin to make dangerous assumptions about who they are. Did any of this stuff tempt New York City's mayor in 2008 to think that he could get the rules suspended so he could run for a third mayoral term in a two-term system?

Saint Paul offered a valuable precedent when he wrote to Timothy and recited his call from Judaism to Christian faith and apostleship: "I was once a blasphemer and a persecutor and a violent man. . . . The grace of our Lord was poured out on me abundantly" (1 Tim. 1:13–14 NIV). A man with a memory like that, regularly freshened, is not likely to think of himself more highly than he ought.

Called People Possess an Unwavering Sense of Purpose

A third look at John's remarkable response to his interrogators will reveal that the prophet from the desert also understood the purpose of his activity as forerunner to Christ. And this is another dimension of calledness. To those who questioned him regarding his feelings about the growing popularity of the Man from Nazareth, he likened his purpose to that of the best man at a wedding: "He who has the bride is the bridegroom; but the friend

LIVING AS A CALLED PERSON

[that's John] of the bridegroom, who stands and hears him, rejoices greatly because of the bridegroom's voice" (John 3:29). The purpose of the best man is simply to stand with the groom, to make sure that all attention is riveted on him. The best man would be a fool if in the middle of the wedding processional he suddenly turned to the wedding guests and began to sing a song or engage in a humorous monologue. The best man has fulfilled his purpose most admirably when he draws no attention to himself but focuses all attention on the bride and groom.

And that is what John did. If Jesus Christ was the groom, to use John's metaphor, then the baptizer was committed to being best man *and nothing else.* That was the purpose that flowed from his call, and he had no desire to aspire to anything beyond. Thus, to see the crowd headed toward Christ was all the affirmation John needed; his purpose had been fulfilled. But only called people, like this man, can relax under such circumstances.

I have long-loved Robert Browning's lines in his poem, "Bishop Bloughram's Apology":

> In everyman's career are certain points
> Whereon he dares not be indifferent;
> The world detects him clearly, if he dare,
> As baffled at the game and losing life.

Among the things we can say about John is this: he was never baffled, and he never lost life. Hard to do if your purpose is lofty and imaginative, if it calls from you every ounce of moral and spiritual energy you have, if it is bigger than you are.

When the 9/11 catastrophe destroyed New York's Trade Towers, my wife, Gail, and I headed for Ground Zero to offer ourselves to the work of the Salvation Army. During that first week when all seemed so chaotic, we were part of the thousands of workers and their relief supports who searched through the rubble in hopes that we would find trapped people still alive.

By the hour, I worked as part of a team that brought everything from cold water to fresh boots to the men and women who formed the bucket brigades intent on getting to anyone who had survived. Occasionally we would hear the signal that meant "silence" as the suspicion arose that a voice or tapping was heard underneath the concrete and steel.

Late one night I stood in a circle of firefighters who had been working 24/7, refusing to rest.

"Don't you think you'd profit from a few hours away from this place?" I asked.

"Not a chance," their leader said. "We've got brothers in that pile, and they may be waiting for us." There was a sense of *call* in those words.

It was moments like this that would cause me to occasionally find Gail at the station where she was dispensing aid, walk off to a corner with her, take her into my arms, and whisper, "I was made for this!"

We both agreed: if anything bad happens—a building falls, the air is found to be toxic with dangerous chemicals—we would not run. We would stay with what we were doing. If it was our time to die, we would accept that as the price for being part of a mission—a call much greater than us.

Now I have a slight, momentary sense of how the great saints—John the Baptizer included—must have continually felt as they lived down through the centuries, caught up in a lofty sense of purpose.

Called People Practice Unswerving Commitment

Finally, John, as a called man, also understood that some things need to be released. Mothers know they must eventually release their children to a more independent life. Mentors know they must release their protégés at an appropriate moment.

John's comment, "He must increase, but I must decrease" (John 3:30), spoken to those who had queried him about his attitude, illustrates the principle of planned release. A called person—because he is a steward, because he knows who he is, because he is purposeful—anticipates the day when it is time to step back and let go. In this case, it was a crowd, a temporary reputation, and a bevy of disciples that had to be released to Jesus' influence.

No driven person could ever say what John said because driven people have to keep gaining more and more attention, more and more power, more and more material assets. They have to hold on; they cannot let go. Too much of themselves is wound up in what they are doing.

Occasionally we hear the story of an organizational leader who, having given powerful leadership to an institution, comes toward the end of his working life and keeps holding on to leadership long after he should have let it pass into the hands of someone in a younger generation. Or he ensures that the leadership passes into the hands of a son or a daughter so that he can maintain his influence.

Somewhere in my library is a book in which the story is told of an English headmaster who was appointed when he was forty-five years of age. His first act was to write himself a letter to be opened on his sixty-fifth birthday. In it he wrote (and I paraphrase), "Today you are sixty-five, and it is time to give the task of being headmaster over to a younger person. You will tell yourself that there is no one who can replace you; that the school cannot do without you. But don't believe this self-aggrandizing propaganda."

Sure enough, when he turned sixty-five and opened the letter, he found that he entertained those exact feelings about his indispensability. But he took his own advice and released the leadership to another. Which is exactly what John did.

It is these kinds of qualities—John's sense of stewardship, his awareness of his identity, his perspective about his role, and his commitment to the principle of release—that mark a called person. And they are the characteristics of a person who builds first in the interior or private world so that out of it will flow fountains of life.

How totally different were the lives of Saul the king and John the Baptizer. The one sought to hold on to what was not his; the other was pleased to use what he was loaned and to return it when it was time.

We can sense a maturity in John's thinking that is uncommon. There's a *peacefulness* about him. This is not a rattled man whose sense of well-being craters when his public world changes.

There's a quality of *joy* that ought not to be confused with the modern-day version of happiness—a state of feelings dependent on everything turning out all right. When others thought that John might be worried about ending up as a failure, they discovered that he actually was quite satisfied, in spite of the fact that his audiences were leaving him. Some folk in John's generation might not have thought so, but John had such an assurance because his evaluations were based first on his private world, where real values can be fully formed in concert with God.

THE ROAD TO CALLEDNESS

As I look with admiration at John the Baptizer, the obvious questions are: How did he get that way? What was the source of this determination, this stamina, this unswerving ability to look at events in a totally different way than others did? A quick overview of John's background offers some insights into the structure and substance of his inner life.

If there is one thing that begins to explain John, it has to be the kind of parents he had, who shaped him in his earliest days. He had good genes—physically and spiritually.

It is clear from Scripture that Zacharias and Elizabeth were godly people with extraordinary sensitivity to John's call. It had been revealed to them through various angelic visions. And they, in turn, from the earliest days began to pump that destiny into John's soul. We have little indication of John's family life after he was born, but we do know that his parents were marked with an extraordinary depth of integrity, godliness, and perseverance.

John's parents must have died when he was still a very young man. How he handled the loss we do not know. But when the Scripture next highlights John, he is living alone in the desert, separate from the society to which he would later speak as a prophet.

> In the fifteenth year of the reign of Tiberius Caesar, when Pontius Pilate was governor of Judea, and Herod was tetrarch of Galilee, and his brother Philip was tetrarch of the region of Ituraea and Trachonitis, and Lysanias was tetrarch of Abilene, in the high priesthood of Annas and Caiaphas, the word of God came to John, the son of Zacharias, in the wilderness. And he came into all the district around the Jordan, preaching a baptism of repentance for the forgiveness of sins. (Luke 3:1–3)

These words contain an intriguing insight. Caesar, we're reminded, was in Rome doing whatever important things Caesars do. Annas and Caiaphas, major-league priests, were in the Jerusalem temple promoting organized religion. And various other political personalities were going and coming in public places, participating in seemingly newsworthy events. Their worlds were the impressive public worlds of power, notoriety, and human connection.

Then this: but *the word of God came to John*, an insignificant man in the most insignificant of places: a desert. Why John? And why a desert? Think about it!

I am reminded of Herbert Butterfield's words, which have always humbled me:

> Both in history and in life it is a phenomenon by no means rare to meet with comparatively unlettered people who seem to have struck profound spiritual depths . . . while there are many highly educated people of whom one feels that they are performing clever antics with their minds to cover a gaping hollowness that lies within.[2]

So why John? First answer: only the God of the round table knows. Beyond that, one simply has to say because John responded. The call demanded submission to God's ways, God's methods, and God's criteria for success. And John was willing to accept those terms, no matter what the cost to him in pain or loneliness.

Why a desert? Perhaps because in deserts people can hear and brood on things not easily heard or thought about in busy cities, where people are usually hurried, surrounded by noise, and steeped in self-importance. Sometimes in cities the shrillness of the public life is so great that the whispering voice of God cannot be heard. And sometimes in cities, people are too proud to listen to God amid all of their steel and concrete skyscrapers, their colorful theaters, or their incredible temples.

God drew John into the desert where He could speak to him. And when He got him there He began to stamp impressions onto John's inner world that gave the son of Zacharias a totally different perspective on his times. There in the desert he gained a new view of religion, of right and wrong, of God's purposes for history. And there he developed a special sensitivity and courage that would

58

prepare him for his most extraordinary task: introducing his generation to the Christ. His private world was under construction—in the desert.

The word of God came to John in the desert. Such a strange place for God to speak. What can a person learn in deserts? I am inclined to forsake deserts, to detour around them whenever possible. To me, deserts mean pain, isolation, and suffering. And no one cares for any of that. Deserts are hard places in which to live, physically or spiritually. But the fact is unavoidable: the greatest lessons are potentially learned in deserts if one, in the midst of struggle, listens for God's call.

In deserts one learns about *dryness* because deserts are dry. Not only would John learn to cope with the dryness of the desert, but it doubtless taught him to appreciate the aridity of the spirits of the people to whom he'd speak at the Jordan.

In the desert a person learns *dependence* on God. Life in the wilderness, as the Hebrews had found out centuries before, cannot be sustained without the benevolence of a merciful God. Only a person who has suffered desert-like hardship knows what it is like to totally cast himself on God because there is nothing else left.

There is a slightly brighter side to deserts, however. Wilderness provides a place where one is free to think, to plan, to prepare. And then at an appointed time, like John, he comes charging out of the dry land with a message, something to say that will expose hypocrisy and superficiality. Issues are addressed that cut through to the bottomless depths of the human spirit. And an age of people is introduced to the Christ of God.

In the desert a person can be called. As John stood up first to his critics, and then to the furiously defensive Herod, whose immoral life the prophet rebuked, he began to reveal that special quality of calledness. You can see it in his serenity in the midst of his prophetic performance. Something special within was operating, providing him with an independent base of judgment and wisdom. Few could withstand his message.

What was the makeup of that private world that was formed in the desert? Frankly, the biblical writers do not give us much of an answer. We are simply treated to the evidence of an ordered inner life. John is a prototype of the product we are looking for. In a public world where all seems chaotic and disordered, he moves with assurance and certitude.

Have Saul, John, and my friend the "successful loser" taught us anything? I think their message is plain. Look inside, they say. What makes you tick? Why are you doing all of that? What do you hope to gain as a result? And what would be your reaction if it were all taken away?

I look inside my private world and discover that almost every day I have to wrestle with whether I will be a Saul or a John. I have lived in a competitive world where achievement is almost everything. Now, as I journey through my seventies, the challenge has morphed a bit. I am (thankfully) no longer an institutional leader. Younger generations are coming behind with better ideas, greater visions, a fresh view of Jesus. Let them carry the burdens that come with institutional leadership.

———

One day not too many years ago, I came to a startling insight. An inner voice seemed to say, *What is the call by which you are living today?*

I suddenly realized that I had spent a large part of my adult life living in response to a call that came to me in my early twenties. But that call—given my age—was no longer compelling.

"Lord," I began to pray each day, "is there a fresh call for a man in the last quarter of his life? Do you have something new for me?"

Every day I prayed this prayer. Weeks went by, and then came an opportunity to spend several days with groups of pastors in Germany. As the days passed and I gave talks in various German cities, younger men frequently approached me and said something like, "When you spoke today, I heard a father's voice."

Returning home to America, I heard the same comment several more times. "You talk to us like a father." And then there was this from the host of a conference where I'd been asked to give some talks: "As Gordon was talking to us, I found myself often on the edge of tears. Now the tears were not because Gordon is a bad speaker. Rather, I felt like I was listening to a father . . . and so many of us in this room feel fatherless."

As I heard these words, I sensed the voice of God's Spirit speaking deep within me. *You wanted a new call? You've got it. Spend the rest of your life being a father to younger men and women who seek a father's voice.*

I have been living out that call for several years now. It is among the greatest calls an old guy can receive. *Don't compete, don't bore people with stories they haven't asked to hear, don't brag about your past. Just listen, encourage, cheer, offer your opinion (when asked), and be ready with a prayer for those who seek a blessing.*

This may sound sort of noble, but it's not always that simple. I have always enjoyed being in charge, more or less. I could still be tempted to join Saul and try to hold on to that which God wants me to surrender. But I prefer to be like John, to release those things that are in the past and embrace those things that are in the future in the freshness of a called life.

Once again, the round table—remember it?—has moved.

SIX

HAS ANYONE SEEN MY TIME? I'VE MISPLACED IT!

I HAD JUST FINISHED A LECTURE TO A GROUP OF PASTORS IN WHICH I mentioned several books I'd read recently. When the talk was finished, a young pastor asked, "Where do you find the time to read all of those books? When I entered the pastorate, I was sure I was going to be able to do that kind of reading too. But I haven't read anything for weeks now. I'm just too swamped!"

We talked for a short while about the discipline of reading, and the conversation began to branch out into other aspects of his personal life. He shared his guilt about his spiritual exercises; they were almost nonexistent. He admitted that it had been a long time since he had spent anything approaching quality time with his wife. He bemoaned the fact that his sermons were usually substandard by his own evaluation. And at the conclusion of our conversation, he conceded that his failure even to read a book was merely the hint of an even bigger struggle. "Frankly," he said, "I'm totally disorganized. I'm not getting anything of consequence done."

I am very sympathetic with this young man and his admission. There was a time in my own life when I could have said the same thing. And I don't think we would have discovered we were the only ones if our colleagues at that lecture had been honest.

The world is full of disorganized people who have lost control of their time.

Ours can be a wordy religion, meaning that one can go a long way, impress a lot of people, simply through a facility with words. It becomes easy to make promises, verbalize intentions, and express one's convictions with seeming passion. But behind the talk can be a lot of wasted time and energy. So we sometimes meet people who do not keep their promises, finish what they start, or back up their verbal intensity with dependable performance. Reason: they do not know how to match their time with appropriate performance.

William Barclay, commenting on the undisciplined life of Samuel Taylor Coleridge, wrote:

> Coleridge is the supreme tragedy of indiscipline. Never did so great a mind produce so little. He left Cambridge University to join the army; he left the army because he could not rub down a horse; he returned to Oxford and left without a degree. He began a paper called *The Watchman*, which lived for ten numbers and then died. It has been said of him: "He lost himself in visions of work to be done, that always remained to be done. Coleridge had every poetic gift but one—the gift of sustained and concentrated effort." In his head and in his mind he had all kinds of books, as he said, himself, "completed save for transcription. I am on the even," he says, "of sending to the press two octavo volumes." But the books were never composed outside Coleridge's mind, because he would not face the discipline of sitting down to write them out. No one ever reached any eminence, and no one having reached it ever maintained it, without discipline.[1]

Coleridge was living proof that a man or woman may be multitalented, possess enormous intelligence and remarkable communicative gifts, and yet end up squandering it all because of an inability to seize control of time. Coleridge's futile pursuits in the literary world are mirrored by some whose vocation is in the home, in the church, or at the office.

None of us, I am sure, wants to come to the end of his or her life and look back with regrets on things that could have been accomplished but were not, as happened to Coleridge. But to prevent that from happening, it is necessary to understand how we can command the time God has given to us.

SYMPTOMS OF DISORGANIZATION

The first step we may have to take is that of a ruthless self-appraisal about our habits of time use. Are we disorganized or not? Let us consider the traits of a disorganized life. Some of these symptoms may seem a bit ridiculous, even petty. But they are usually part of a larger picture that all fits together. Let me suggest a handful of sample symptoms.

When I am slipping into a state of disorganization, for example, I know it because my desk takes on a cluttered appearance. The same thing happens to the top of my bedroom dresser. In fact, almost every horizontal surface in the path of my daily travel becomes littered with papers, memos to which I have not responded, and bits of tasks that are unfinished. I can see some spouse saying, "Here, read this; he's been in your office lately." But my desk can be another's kitchen counter, workbench, or basement workroom. The same principle applies.

The symptoms of disorganization tend to show themselves in the condition of my car. It becomes dirty inside and out. I lose track of its maintenance schedule, and I find that I am pressing deadlines for things like changing snow tires and getting the annual safety sticker.

When disorganization takes over, I become aware of a diminution in my self-confidence. I feel the slightest tinge of paranoia, a low-level fear that people are going to discover they are not getting their money's worth out of my labor, that they are going to conclude that I am not half the man they thought I was.

I know I'm disorganized when there are a series of forgotten appointments, telephone messages to which I have failed to respond, and deadlines I have begun to miss. The day becomes filled with broken commitments and lame excuses. (I must be careful to say, incidentally, that I am not thinking of times when events beyond my control have conspired to derail even the best intentions. All of us have those kinds of days, even the most organized of us.)

If I am disorganized, I tend to invest my energies in unproductive tasks. I find myself doing small and boring things just to get something accomplished. There is a tendency toward daydreaming, avoidance of decisions that have to be made, and procrastination. Disorganization begins to affect every part of my will to work steadily and excellently.

DISORGANIZED PEOPLE FEEL POORLY ABOUT THEIR WORK. What they manage to finish, they do not like. They find it very hard to accept the compliments of others. In the secrecy of their hearts they know that they have turned in a second-best job.

I have more than once driven home from Sunday morning worship services where I have preached in this sort of mood. And as I drove, I found myself pounding the steering wheel in frustration because I knew that I could have preached better if I had used my time during the week more effectively in study and preparation.

DISORGANIZED CHRISTIANS RARELY ENJOY INTIMACY WITH GOD. They certainly have intentions of pursuing that camaraderie, but it never quite gets established. No one has to tell them that time must be set aside for the purpose of Bible study and reflection, for intercession, for worship. They know all of that. They simply are not doing it. They excuse themselves, saying there is no time, but within their private worlds they know it is more a matter of organization and personal will than anything else.

If I am in a state of disorganization, the quality of my personal relationships usually reveals it. The days pass without a significant conversation with my son or daughter. My wife and I will be in contact, but our conversations may be shallow, devoid of self-revelation, and unaffirming. I may become irritable, resenting any attempt on her part to call to my attention things I have left undone or people I appear to have let down.

The fact of the matter is that when we are disorganized in our control of time, we just don't like ourselves, our jobs, or much else about our worlds. And it is difficult to break the destructive pattern that settles in.

This terrible habit of disorganization must be broken, or our private worlds will fall quickly into total disorder. We must resolve to seize control of our time.

Psychologists can suggest many reasons for people's being disorganized, and it is helpful to think some of these through. There is a large body of helpful literature available on the subject of time management and organization. But beneath the gimmicks and tricks of organization are some fundamental principles that must be seriously considered by any person seeking an ordering of the private world. Putting these principles into practice will be a challenge for some men and women who have ignored the importance of controlling their time.

BUDGETING TIME

The central principle of all personal organization of time is simple: *time must be budgeted!*

Most of us learned this about money a long time ago. When we discovered that we rarely had enough money to do all the things we wanted to do with it, we found it prudent to sit down and think through our financial priorities.

With money, the priorities were obvious. Since my wife and I are committed to God's plan of stewardship, our first financial priority has always been our tithe and offerings. Then the fixed expenditures of food, house, utilities, books (both of us insist that books are a fixed expenditure), and so on have been set aside in amounts that we have learned to anticipate.

Only after we have budgeted these amounts of money for the necessities have we ventured into the discretionary side of the budget, namely those things that are more wants than needs. Here we may be talking about a meal out at a favorite restaurant, an appliance that makes life a bit easier, or a particularly attractive winter coat.

When men and women do not understand the difference between the fixed and the discretionary aspects of their financial lives, they usually end up in debt, which is the financial version of disorganization.

When money is limited, one budgets. And when time is in limited supply, the same principle holds. The disorganized person must have a budgeting perspective. And that means determining the difference between the fixed—what one must do—and the discretionary—what one *would like* to do.

These were the items I raised when my young pastor friend came to talk about why he felt so unproductive. He was surprised when I told him that we were talking about one of my own daily battles.

"Gordon," he said, "you don't convey the impression that time is ever out of your control."

I protested, "I sometimes wonder if I've ever got any of it under control." All of those symptoms of the disorganized life were at one time or another my symptoms, but I had made a decision (actually on more than one occasion) that I was not going to live that way for one more minute than I had to.

THE LORD OF TIME

My young pastor friend was obviously hoping I would share with him a few of the insights that have challenged me to order my private world in the area of time use. If he thought I had a bag of answers that would make it easy, he was to be disappointed. As our conversation continued, I suggested that he take a hard look at one Person who never seems to have wasted a moment.

When I look in the Bible, I am deeply impressed with the practical lessons on organization that one can learn from the life and work of Jesus Christ. All four gospel writers present to us a picture of Jesus under constant pressure, as He was pursued by friend and enemy alike. His every word was monitored, every action was analyzed, every gesture was commented on. Essentially, Jesus had no private life to speak of.

I have tried to imagine our Lord in today's world. Would He carry a pager or a cell phone? Would He fly, drive, or take the train? Would He be drawn to direct-mail campaigns? How would He handle the huge number of relationships that modern technology has made it possible for us to maintain? How would He fit in to a time where a word spoken can be flashed around the world in seconds to become headlines for the next morning's paper?

Although His everyday world was on a much smaller scale, it seems He lived with very much the same sort of intrusions and demands with which we are familiar. But one never gets the feeling, when studying the life of Christ, that He ever hurried, that He ever had to play catch-up, or that He was ever taken by surprise. Not only was He adept at handling His public time without an appointments secretary, but He also managed adequate amounts of time alone for prayer and meditation, and for being with the few He had gathered around Him for the purpose of discipleship. Again, all this was made possible because He had brought His time under control.

It is worth taking time to ask how our Lord's command of time is demonstrated. What caused Him to be such an organized person?

The first thing that impresses me is that *Jesus clearly understood His mission*. He had an overarching task to perform, and He measured His use of time against that sense of mission. This is quite apparent during His final walk toward Jerusalem, where He would be crucified. As Jesus approached Jericho, Luke wrote (chapter 18), His ears picked up the shrill voice of a blind man and He stopped, much to the consternation of both His friends and critics. They were irritated that Jesus did not appreciate that Jerusalem was still six or seven hours away, and that they would like to get there to achieve their purpose, the celebration of Passover.

And, indeed, they had a point—the purpose of Christ was merely to reach Jerusalem in time for a religious celebration. But as we soon learn, that was not Jesus' prime mission. Touching broken people like the blind man was a more significant matter, important enough for Jesus to invest His time.

Not long after the first encounter, Jesus stopped once again, this time under the branch of a tree to call down Zacchaeus, a well-known tax collector. It was the Lord's idea that the two get together for a conversation at Zacchaeus's house. Once again the crowd surrounding Jesus was incensed, first because the trip to Jerusalem was again interrupted, and second because of Zacchaeus's reputation.

From where they were standing, it appeared that Jesus was misusing His time. From where Jesus was standing, however, the time was well spent, for it fit the criteria of His mission.

Luke recorded the words of Jesus about this very fact: "The

Son of Man has come to seek and to save that which was lost" (Luke 19:10). The disciples had a difficult time understanding this, and Jesus had to constantly confront them with the specific facts of His mission. Until they owned that mission, they would never understand how and with what criteria He organized His time.

A second insight into Jesus' personal organization of time is that *He understood His own limits.* When Jesus came to earth as the incarnate Son of God, He set aside certain rights as the Prince of heaven and accepted, for a time, certain human limitations in order to fully identify with us. He shared our limitations, but He coped with them effectively—just as we must.

We dare not minimize the fact that Jesus sought time in solitude with the heavenly Father before every important decision and action during His public ministry.

There are thirty years of virtual silence before Jesus went public with His mission. Only when we are treated to an audience with Christ in eternity will we fully understand the importance of those three decades. At best, we can now conclude that they were a significant time of preparation. It is impressive to realize that there were thirty years of relative obscurity and privacy in preparation for three years of important activity.

We should not be surprised, then, that Moses spent forty years in the desert before confronting Pharaoh. Paul spent an extensive amount of time in the desert listening to God before assuming apostolic duties. And the experience of these men was not exceptional.

Just before Jesus assumed public ministry, He spent forty days in the wilderness communing with the Father. Don't forget the night spent in prayer before the choosing of the Twelve. There was an early-morning vigil on the mountainside the day after a busy time in Capernaum. And, of course, there was the withdrawal to the Mount of Transfiguration to prepare for the final trek to Jerusalem. Finally, there was Gethsemane.

Jesus knew His limits well. Strange as it may seem, He knew what we conveniently forget: *time must be properly budgeted for the gathering of inner strength and resolve in order to compensate for one's weaknesses when spiritual warfare begins.* Such private moments were a fixed item on Jesus' time budget because He knew His limits. And it was very hard even for those closest to Him to fully appreciate this.

I think Jesus included a third important element in His strategy of time budgeting, for *He set time aside for the training of the Twelve.* With a world of millions to reach, Jesus budgeted the majority of His time to be with just a few simple men.

Prime time was invested in taking them through the Scriptures and sharing His heavenly insights. Key moments were spent sharing ministry with individuals and permitting them to watch every action and hear every word. Special days were set aside to explain to them the deeper meanings of His talks to the crowds. And valuable hours were seized in order to debrief them when they returned from assignments, to rebuke them when they failed, and to affirm them when they succeeded.

We might have been tempted to ask more than once why Jesus was spending so much valuable time with a group of simple-minded men when He could have taught men who could have intellectually appreciated His theological expertise. But Jesus was aware of where true importance lies, where the priorities are. And where your priorities are, there your time will be.

For reasons like these, Jesus was never to be caught short on time. He knew His sense of mission, He was spiritually sharpened by moments alone with the Father, and He knew who the men were who would perpetuate His mission long after He ascended into heaven. It was never difficult for Him to say a firm no to invitations and demands that might have looked good or acceptable to us.

There came a time in my own life when my study of Jesus made me deeply desire this capacity. I wanted to make sound decisions about the budgeting of my time, and I wanted to be free of that frantic pitch of daily life in which one is always playing catch-up. Was it possible? Not the way I was going!

The young pastor who had come to me at the end of my lecture remained very interested. I suggested that we get together on another day. Perhaps there would be some practical things I could share with him. But I would have to be brutally honest with him. I learned most of them the hard way.

SEVEN

RECAPTURING MY TIME

THE YOUNG PASTOR AND I WERE TO RESUME OUR CONVERSATION SOME days later. In the interim, I began gathering thoughts about what I had learned over the past few years that had helped me begin getting my own life together in this area. What had I learned through the experience of failure, and what had I learned in talking with others in the same way that this young man was coming to talk with me?

The more I looked at the lessons learned, the more I realized how important it is to gain control of time as early in life as possible. Putting them down on paper, I discovered that there were only a few basic principles. But until those were mastered, the time issue would always be big and potentially discouraging. What I found myself writing down in preparation for my next conversation was something I came to call "MacDonald's Laws of Unmanaged Time." Here is what I collected.

MACDONALD'S LAWS OF UNMANAGED TIME

Law #1: Unmanaged Time Flows Toward My Weaknesses

Because I had not adequately defined a sense of mission in the early days of my work, and because I had not been ruthless enough with my weaknesses, I found that I normally invested inordinately large amounts of time doing things I was not good at, while the tasks I should have been able to do with excellence and effectiveness were preempted.

I know many Christian leaders who feel that they spend up to 60 percent of their time (perhaps a lot more, actually) doing things at which they are second best. For example, I am an idea person. I am comfortable thinking, as they say, outside the box; I am not disturbed by ambiguity; I have a nose for patterns and trendlines. Beyond that, I enjoy challenging the status quo. That sort of strength gets fleshed out as a preacher, a teacher, and a consultant of sorts. It offers a form of organizational leadership as a visionary—someone who sees possibilities a second or two before others might see them.

But this capability demands large blocks of time for reading, studying, and reflecting. In the earlier days of Polaroid, when Dr. Edwin Land, its founder, was in his prime, the Polaroid people saw that he could be of supreme value to the company if he was excused from running the company on a day-to-day basis and given a research lab where he could use his mighty gift to come up with new concepts that would result in new products. It was a splendid idea, and everyone won as a result.

The churches I have pastored rarely saw that there might be a similar value—as an idea person—in me, so they tended to insist that I invest a lot of my time doing things at which I am less than best: namely, people management and administration. So I did it, made a choice to enjoy it, but rarely felt satisfied that I was giving the organization my best.

Why did I spend almost 75 percent of my available time trying to administrate and relatively little time studying and preparing to preach good sermons when I was younger? Unseized time will flow in the direction of one's relative weakness. Since I knew I could preach an acceptable sermon with a minimum of preparation, I was doing less than my best in the pulpit. That is what happens when one does not evaluate this matter and do something drastic about it.

So I did the drastic thing. I sought the aid of a few sensitive men who cared enough to help me face what was happening and to show me how I might be squandering my potential. With their help I made a decision to delegate the administration of our congregation's ministry to a competent administrative pastor. It was not easy at first because I was in the habit of offering an opinion on every decision. Now I had to back off and leave that in someone else's hands. But it worked! And when I could fully trust our administrative pastor (which I soon found easy to do), I was able to redirect a great amount of energy into things that, God willing, I am most likely to do well.

I can almost hear someone say, "That's fine if the money is available to hire someone to compensate for my weaknesses." And, perhaps in some cases, the only help these comments may offer is to make us realize *why* we are frustrated when time seems to escape us. But I must add that it may be more possible than we realize to find creative ways to share tasks with others. First, we must sit ourselves down and consider who is best at doing what. This applies in the home, in the office, and in the church.

Law #2: Unmanaged Time Comes Under the Influence of Dominant People in My World

A famous "spiritual law" states that "God loves you and has a plan for your life." Men and women who do not have control of their time discover that the same can be said about dominating people.

Because they have not set up their own time budgets, people succumbing to this law find that others enter their worlds and press agendas and priorities on them. As a young pastor, I discovered that because my time was not fully organized, I was at the mercy of anyone who had a notion to visit or take me to coffee or who wanted my attendance at a committee meeting. Since my calendar was disorganized, how could I say no? Especially when, as a young man, I was eager to please people.

Not only was I deprived of my best time due to this lack of organization, but my family was often cheated out of precious hours that I should have given them. And so it continued. Strong people in my world controlled my time better than I did because I had not taken the initiative to command the time before they got to me. This sometimes led to resentment toward them and disrespect toward myself. Not a good way to live.

Law #3: Unmanaged Time Surrenders to the Demands of All Emergencies

Charles Hummel, writing years ago in a small and classic booklet, said it best: we are governed by the tyranny of the urgent. Those of us with any sort of responsibility for leadership, whether in our vocations, homes, or faith, will find ourselves continually surrounded by events that cry out for immediate attention.

One summer, when our associate pastor and I were both on vacation, one of our staff members took a phone call from a church member who wanted me to preside at the funeral of a distant relative of his. When told that I was away for the month, he asked for my associate and was disappointed to discover that he was also gone. He was offered the services of one of the other pastors on the staff, but he refused, saying, "No, I won't go any lower than number two."

His thinking was the sort that creates urgent situations for leaders. Everyone would like the attention of the number-one person. Every committee and board would like the number-one person to attend their meetings, even if they do not always wish to hear his opinions. Most people in any sort of trouble would like the immediate response of the number-one leader.

One Saturday afternoon the phone rang in our home, and when I answered, the woman's voice at the other end of the line sounded quite upset. "I've got to see you right away," she said. When I learned her name, I quickly realized that I had never met this person before and that she had rarely ever visited our church.

"What is the reason that we have to visit right now?" I asked. It was an important question, one of several I've learned through experience to ask. Had this been many years ago when I was young, I would have responded immediately to her sense of emergency and arranged to meet her in ten minutes at my office, even if I had previously hoped to be with the family or involved with study.

"My marriage is breaking up," she responded. I then asked, "When did you become aware that it was going to break up?"

She answered, "Last Tuesday." I asked another question. "How long do you think the process of breaking up has been going on?" Her next comment was unforgettable.

"Oh, it's been coming for several years." I managed to stifle my real reaction and said, "Since you've seen this coming for so many years, and since you knew it was going to happen since last Tuesday, why is it important to visit with me right at this moment? I need to know that."

She answered, "Oh, I had some free time this afternoon and just thought it might be a good time to get together with you."

Law number three would usually mean that I would have surrendered to her desire to see me immediately. But by this point in my life, most of my time was accounted for; so I said, "I can understand why you think you have a serious problem. Now I'm going to be very candid with you. I have to speak three times tomorrow morning, and frankly my mind is preoccupied with that responsibility. Since you've been living with this situation for several years now, and since you've had several days to think about it, I'm going to propose that you call me on Monday morning so we can arrange a time when my mind is in much better shape. I want to be able to give you the utmost in concentration. But that's probably not possible this afternoon. How does that sound?"

She thought it was a terrific idea and could see why I would suggest that sort of plan. Both of us hung up reasonably happy: she, knowing she would eventually get to talk to me; me, because I had reserved my time for the matter that was most important on that Saturday afternoon. A seemingly urgent thing had not broken through the time budget. Not everything that cries the loudest is the most urgent thing.

In his spiritual autobiography (one of my favorites), *While It Is Day*, Elton Trueblood wrote:

> A public man, though he is necessarily available at many times, must learn to hide. If he is always available, he is not worth enough when he is available. I once wrote a chapter in the Cincinnati Union Station, but that was itself a form of hiding because nobody knew who the man with the writing pad was. Consequently nobody approached me during five wonderful hours until the departure of the next train to Richmond. *We must use the time which we have because even at best there is never enough.*[1]

Trueblood's comments, seemingly dated, are as fresh today as the moment he wrote them years ago.

Law #4: Unmanaged Time Gets Invested in Things That Gain Public Acclamation

In other words, we are more likely to give our unbudgeted time to events that will bring the most immediate and greatest praise.

When Gail and I were first married, we found that we could attract a lot of invitations to banquets and meetings of various sorts, if we were willing to sing solos and duets. It was nice to receive the warm applause and gain the popularity. But the performance of music was not our call or our priority. Preaching and pastoral care were. Unfortunately, young preachers were not (and rarely are) in great demand, and the temptation was to do anything that would make us attractive to people.

We had to make a critical decision. Would we involve our time in doing what people most liked for us to do? Or would we buckle down and give our attention to what was most important: learning the ways of preaching and counseling? Fortunately, we chose to avoid the seduction of the former and embrace the latter. It paid off.

We have had to make choices like that throughout our married life. And more than once I have made the wrong choice. There was a time when it seemed glamorous to fly across the country to speak at a banquet. But it was a poor use of time. The old comment "A sermon is something I'd go across the country to preach but not across the street to hear" is too close to the truth to be comfortable. It once seemed enchanting to be at the head table of some politician's prayer breakfast or to be interviewed on a Christian radio program, but it may not have been a high-priority use of time.

Thus, the laws of unmanaged time come back to haunt the disorganized person again and again, until he decides to gain the initiative before everyone and every event does it for him.

RECAPTURING LOST TIME

In gathering material for that upcoming conversation with the young pastor, I looked back on my own experience, trying to identify the principles that, when implemented, brought some order into my private world. And when I thought hard about the process that I had come through, I found that I was able to come up with three ways of successfully recapturing time.

1. I Must Know My Rhythms of Maximum Effectiveness

A careful study of my work habits has revealed to me an important insight. There are various tasks I accomplish best at certain times and under certain conditions.

For example, I have never studied effectively for Sunday sermons during the early days of the week. Two hours of study on Monday were relatively worthless, but one hour (and hopefully a lot more) on Thursday or Friday was almost priceless. I simply concentrate better. On the other hand, during the early days of the week, I am at my best with people, when the tension of anticipated preaching has not yet grabbed my mind. I tend to diminish in effectiveness with people later in the week, when I become preoccupied with Sunday's pulpit experience.

I can fine-tune that observation even further. What study time I do take is best taken early in the morning, when I have reasonable amounts of unbroken solitude. And "people time" for me is best taken in the afternoon, when I feel reflective and insightful.

Learning about my rhythms has taught me to reserve study time for the last half of the week and plan time with people and committees as much as possible in the first part of the week. In this way, my time budget reflects and uses the rhythms of my life.

I have also taken notice of the fact that I am a morning person. I can rise early and be quite alert if I have gone to bed at a reasonable hour the night before. So it is important to me to maintain a fairly standard bedtime. We enforced that principle with our children when they were young. I don't know why it never dawned on us that a standard bedtime as much as possible was probably a wise thing for us as adults. And when I finally saw this, I tried to go to bed at the same time each night.

After reading an article by a specialist on the subject of sleep, I began to experiment to find out how much sleep I needed. The writer suggested that one can determine his sleep requirements by setting his alarm for a certain hour and rising at that time for three mornings in a row. Then the alarm should be set ten minutes earlier for the next three days. By so continuing in three-day increments, setting the alarm back ten minutes in each period, one will finally come to a natural fatigue point, where throughout the following day he does not feel properly rested. I tried it, found I could rise much earlier than I had thought, and it added almost two full hours—valuable hours—to my day.

There are weekly rhythms, daily rhythms, and annual rhythms. I found that there were certain months of the year when I was apt to face abnormal emotional fatigue, times when part of me wanted to run from people and from responsibility. I had to face up to that. On the other hand, there were times in the year when I had to be relatively stronger as a Christian leader because many people around me were living with too much fatigue and pressure. The months of February and March are times like that, when all of us in New England fight the effects of a long winter and tend toward irritability and a critical spirit. I have learned to prepare myself to be an extra special encouragement to others during those times. And when spring comes and people feel revitalized, then I can enjoy my own private time of letdown. Knowing those things were likely to happen was a great help to me. I could plan for them.

I have learned that the summer months are a fine time for extra reading and for spiritually preparing myself for the coming year. But during January through March, for reasons I have just mentioned, I plan to be with people much of the time because the counseling schedule is likely to jump dramatically. All of my books have been written in the summer months; there is no way they could have been done in winter.

Knowing my rhythms, I am not surprised when I feel inwardly empty after a period of heavy speaking and teaching. I cannot live day after day above the emotional line without coming to a moment when I must dip just a bit beneath the line of emotional normalcy to regather strength that has been lost. Thus, I learned as a pastor that it was wise not to make important decisions on a Monday, after a day of preaching several sermons. And if I had pushed hard, day after day during a holiday season, it was wise for me to plan a short comedown period when it was all over.

I prize a segment in a letter that William Booth, founder of the Salvation Army, once received from his wife when he was on an extensive trip:

> Your Tuesday's notes arrived safe, and I was rejoiced to hear of the continued prosperity of the work, though sorry you were so worn out; I fear the effect of all this excitement and exertion upon your health, and though I would not hinder your usefulness, I would caution you against an injudicious prodigality of your strength.
>
> Remember a long life of steady, consistent, holy labor will produce twice as much fruit as one shortened and destroyed by spasmodic and extravagant exertions; be careful and sparing of your strength when and where exertion is unnecessary.[2]

2. I Must Have Thoughtful Criteria for Choosing How to Use My Time

Years ago my father suggested that one of the great tests of human character is found in making critical choices of selection and rejection amid all of the opportunities that lurk in life's path. "Your challenge," he told me, "will not be in separating out the good from the bad, but in grabbing the *best* out of all the possible good." He was absolutely correct. I did indeed have to learn, sometimes the hard way, that I had to say no to things I really wanted to do in order to say yes to the very best things.

Heeding that counsel often meant saying no to dinner parties and sporting events on Saturday night so I could be fresh mentally and physically on Sunday morning. It meant declining certain speaking dates to which I wanted to say yes.

Sometimes I find such choices hard to make, simply because I like people to approve of me. When a person learns to say no to good things, he or she runs the risk of making enemies and gaining critics; and who needs more of those? So I find it hard to say no.

I have discovered that most people whose lives are leadership centered face the same challenge. But my father's counsel is fool-proof: if we are to command our time, we have to bite the bullet and say a firm but courteous no to opportunities that are merely good but not best.

Once again that demands, as it did in the ministry of our Lord, a sense of our mission. What are we called to do? What do we do best with our time? What are the necessities without which we cannot get along? Everything else must be considered negotiable, discretionary, not necessary.

I am drawn to the words C. S. Lewis wrote in *Letters to an American Lady* about the importance of these choices:

> Don't be too easily convinced that God really wants you to do all sorts of work you needn't do. Each must do his duty "in that state of life to which God has called him." Remember that a belief in the virtues of doing for doing's sake is characteristically feminine, characteristically American, and characteristically modern: so that *three* veils may divide you from the correct view! There can be intemperance in work just as in drink. What feels like zeal may be only fidgets or even the flattering of one's self importance. . . . By doing what "one's station and its duties" does not demand, one can make oneself less fit for the duties it *does* demand and so commit some injustice. Just you give Mary a little chance as well as Martha.[3]

3. I Manage Time and Command It Best When I Budget It Far in Advance

This last principle is the most important; here is where the battle is won or lost.

I have learned the hard way that the principal elements of my time budget have to be in the calendar eight weeks in advance of the date. Eight weeks!

If this is August, then I am already beginning to think through October. And what goes into the calendar? Those non-negotiable aspects of my private world: my spiritual disciplines, my mental disciplines, my sabbath rest, and of course my commitments to family and special friendships. Then a second tier of priorities will enter the calendar: the schedule of the main work to which I am committed—sermon study, writing, leadership development, and discipling.

As much as possible, all of this is placed in the calendar many, many weeks in advance of the target week because as I get closer to that week, I discover that people move in to make demands on the available time. Some of them will have legitimate demands, and it is to be hoped there will be space for them.

But others will make demands that are not appropriate. They will inquire about an evening that I have scheduled for the family. Or they will want an hour in a morning reserved for study. How much better my private world is when I allow these activities to *flow around* the priorities and into available slots than when things are the other way around.

It occurred to me one day that my most important time allocations had something in common. They never screamed out immediately when ignored. I could neglect my spiritual disciplines, for example, and God did not seem to shout about it. I could make it just fine for a while. And when I did not allocate time for the family, Gail and the children were generally understanding and forgiving—often more so than certain church members who demanded instant response and attention. And when I set study aside as a priority, I could get away with it for a while. These things could be ignored for a while without adverse consequences. And that is why they were so often crowded out when I did not budget for them in advance. Other less important issues had a way of wedging them aside week after week. Tragically, if they are neglected too long, when family, rest, and spiritual disciplines are finally noticed, it is often too late for adverse consequences to be avoided.

When our son, Mark, was in high school, he was a successful athlete; our teenage daughter, Kristen, was an actor and musician. Both were in games and performances. It would have been easy to have missed those events had I not penciled the dates into the calendar weeks and weeks in advance. My secretary always kept the game schedules in the office calendar, for example, and knew full well not to expect me to commit to anything that would violate those times.

When someone would ask me to meet with him on the afternoon of a game, I was liable to take out my calendar and stroke my chin thoughtfully, saying, "I'm sorry, I'm unable to do it that day; I already have a commitment. How about this as an alternative?" I rarely had a problem. The key was in planning and budgeting, weeks in advance.

One needs to ask, what are my non-negotiables? I have discovered that most of us who complain that we are disorganized simply do not know the answer to this question. As a result, the important functions that will make the supreme difference in our effectiveness miss getting into the calendar until it is too late. The consequence? Disorganization and frustration; the nonessentials crowd into the date book before the necessities do. And that is painful over the long run.

The other day a man caught up with me and asked if we could

have an early morning breakfast on a certain day. "How early?" I asked.

"You're an early riser," he said. "Why not six?" I looked at my calendar and said, "I'm sorry, I've already got a commitment for that hour; how about seven?" He agreed on seven rather quickly but looked quite surprised that my calendar might reflect plans for that early in the morning.

I did have a commitment for six that morning. In fact, it started earlier than that. It was a commitment to God. He was first on the calendar that day where He belongs every day. And it is not the sort of commitment one compromises. Not if one wants to seize time and keep it under control. It is the start of an organized day, an organized life, and an organized private world.

EIGHT

THE BETTER MAN LOST

ANYONE ACQUAINTED WITH MY WRITING KNOWS THAT I OFTEN SPEAK of the lessons I learned on the track and cross-country course. Although I might have been a more successful runner if I had been tougher on myself, those years of competitive running in prep school and college were nevertheless an opportunity for rich learning experiences in terms of the development of conditioning and character.

Some of the most memorable occasions were at the Penn Relays in Philadelphia. There is one story I have relayed many times.

I had been chosen to be the leadoff man for our prep school mile relay team, a strategically important slot in the running order. My objective was to gain the lead in the race and, when I had completed my quarter-mile leg, hand that advantage on to the second runner on our team.

For me not to be in first place when I approached the hand-off box would mean that our second man would receive the relay baton while caught in a chaotic cluster of runners. If that happened, there was the risk of a loss of stride in the inevitable jostling and shoving. A precious second or two could be easily lost.

Since our team had drawn the number-two lane, I was curious

to see what team had won the "pole," or number-one lane position. It turned out to be the team from Poly Prep, for many years our traditional league rival. Their leadoff man owned an impressive record as a sprinter in the 100-meter dash. He and I had competed against each other on a couple of other occasions at a shorter distance, and he had beaten me rather badly. Would it be the same result when the race was 300 meters longer?

It was obvious that he thought so because he said as much when we shook hands at the starting line. Looking squarely at me, he said, "I'll be waiting for you at the finish line." Today we call that trash talk, a kind of athletic psychological warfare. It partially worked, and for a moment I had to struggle to gain my equilibrium.

The gun went off, and so did the man from Poly Prep. I can remember feeling the sting of the cinders that his spikes shot backward on my shins as he seemed to instantly disappear around the first turn. Meanwhile the remaining seven runners began what looked like a competition for positions number two through eight. Before I had run fifty yards, I began to mentally prepare for finishing in second place, assuming I could make even that happen.

And that is indeed what would have happened—if the race had been shorter. Somewhere around the 300-meter point, however, affairs abruptly changed. The man from Poly Prep, far out in front, suddenly slowed down from sprint to jog. A second later, as I charged around him, now running at my peak stride, I could hear him struggling to breathe. He was barely moving. As athletes put it, he was out of gas. I don't remember in what place he finished, but I do know that I was waiting for him at the finish line, trying hard not to gloat.

I learned a valuable lesson that day at the expense of the man from Poly Prep. Inadvertently, he had taught me that even men and women of great talent and energy have to run the *complete* course before they can claim the victory. To be in front at the first turn is meaningless without the endurance to finish strongly. The race must be run at a steady pace all the way to the finish. And a good runner is even prepared to complete the course with a "kick," an extra burst of speed. Athletic talent is of little consequence unless it is matched to adequate endurance.

THE COST OF MENTAL FLABBINESS

I tell this story because it speaks to another segment of our private lives that must be consistent in the process of personal organization. The ordering of our private world cannot take place without strong mental endurance and the intellectual growth this endurance produces.

In our pressurized society, people who are out of shape mentally usually fall victim to ideas and systems that are destructive to the human spirit and to human relationships. They are victimized because they have not taught themselves how to think, nor have they set themselves to the lifelong pursuit of the growth of the mind. Not having the facility of a strong mind, they grow dependent on the thoughts and opinions of others. Rather than deal with ideas and issues, they reduce themselves to lives full of rules, regulations, and programs.

V. W. Burroughs wrote: "One of the saddest experiences is to awaken at old age and discover that one has been using only a small part of self." He says it quite succinctly. Many of us are always in danger of squandering that enormous wealth of thinking power that God built into humanity at creation. He ordained that we should be *mindful*, not *mindless* people. But mindfulness is a matter of discipline and hard work. Mindlessness is the result of laziness and fear.

Those of us who are older vividly remember the 1978 mass suicide in Guyana by more than nine hundred members of the

Peoples' Temple. It is a poignant example of where mindlessness can lead.

Allowing their "guru-pastor" Jim Jones to do their thinking for them, the community courted disaster. They switched off their minds and depended on the functioning of his. And when Jones's mind ceased working correctly, everyone suffered the consequences. A leader had promised people guidance in the midst of a hostile and angry world. He had offered answers and sustenance. And people signed away their right to independent judgment as the price of such security.

People whose minds are not strengthened for endurance are by no means always unintelligent. They simply have never stopped to think that the use of the mind for the purpose of growth is a necessary part of a God-pleasing lifestyle. It is easy to fall into the trap of allowing the mind to grow flaccid, especially when there are many dominant people all around who would just as soon do our thinking for us.

Such mindlessness can be seen in an unbalanced—and ungodly—family, where one person intimidates all other family members into letting him or her do all the decision-making and opinion-forming. We have many examples of churches where laypeople delegate the thinking to a highly dominant pastor. The epistle of 3 John speaks against a man named Diotrephes, a lay leader who, like Jim Jones, had virtually everyone under his control. The Christians simply surrendered their thinking to him.

THE DANGER OF BEING A FAST STARTER

As in a race I described, where a naturally talented runner springs from the starting blocks with a blinding burst of speed, there are those who enjoy fast starts in adult life—not because they are great thinkers or mental giants, but rather because of natural abilities and useful connections. They may have had the benefit of growing up in talented families, where the people around them were highly communicative and gifted in dealing with ideas and problem-solving. As a result, they may have acquired considerable self-confidence at an early age.

Such early exposures teach the young person how to lead, how to compete against others, and how to handle oneself in difficult situations. The result could be called "premature success." And premature success is often more an obstacle than a help.

The premature succeeder is usually a fast learner, able to acquire expertise with minimum effort. He is usually blessed with good health and abundant energy. He can talk his way into or out of anything, it seems. And he may conclude that he can do just about anything he sets his mind to because things appear to come easily to him.

How long things can go on this way is anyone's guess. For a lifetime, I suppose, in certain cases. But my observation is that somewhere in his early thirties, indications of possible trouble will begin to show in the life of the naturally talented fast starter. There may be the first hints that the rest of the race in life will have to be run on endurance and discipline, not talent. And like the runner from Poly Prep, he may start to see that the slower but better-conditioned runners are beginning to catch up.

In my lifetime I have met many people who are struggling through midlife for this reason. I see a startling number of exhausted, mentally empty people who have stopped growing and are spending their lives in the pursuit of little more than amusement.

I use the word *amusement* because of its literal meaning. It suggests "function without thought" (*a* meaning "without"; and *muse* meaning "to think"). Functioning without thought leads to a feeling of personal disorganization. Who are the people who function without thought? They can easily be folk of whom it was said twenty years before, "He is going places; he can't miss." It can be the preacher who at the age of twenty-one had unusual pulpit powers, the salesman who began his career with a remarkable record of completed deals, the woman who graduated valedictorian of her class. It tends to be those who never realized that the mind must be pushed, filled, stretched, and forced in order to function. Natural talent takes such people only so far and lets them down long before the race is finished.

THE LIFE OF THE MIND

The mind must be *trained* to think, to analyze, to innovate. People fully organized in their private worlds *work* at being thinkers. Their minds are alert and alive, taking on fresh amounts of information every day, regularly producing new discoveries and conclusions. They commit themselves to the daily exercise of the mind.

"I possessed information without knowledge, opinions without principles, instincts without beliefs," wrote *New Yorker* movie critic David Denby when he looked back on his youthful self.[1] That's a scary discovery for a man to make; it is a call to re-evaluate one's way of looking at things. It's what Paul was thinking about when he wrote: "Do not be conformed to this world, but be transformed by the renewing of your mind" (Rom. 12:2).

Paul saw our alternatives very clearly. The person who does not know how to think will be relentlessly shaped and influenced by the dominant culture around him or her. But the transformed person (presumably transformed by the Spirit of Christ) will be busy thinking, reflecting, and making independent conclusions about the meaning of life and reality.

You see this throughout the scriptural stories of great men and women. Esther, who ascended to the position of Persian queen under strange circumstances, was chided by her mentor, Mordecai, when he became aware of a growing plot to wipe out the Jews. When Esther initially resisted his encouragement to confront the king on this matter, he wrote, "Do not imagine that you in the king's palace can escape any more than all the Jews. For if you remain silent at this time, relief and deliverance will arise for the Jews from another place and you and your father's house will perish. And who knows whether you have not attained royalty for such a time as this?" (Est. 4:13–14).

Think, Esther, think! That's Mordecai's message. But what if one has never been trained to think?

"No vital Christianity is possible unless at least three aspects of it are developed," wrote Elton Trueblood. "These three are the inner life of devotion, the outer life of service, and the *intellectual life of rationality*."[2] The third aspect is the easiest for many Christ-followers to ignore, thinking it too worldly (as some like to say) and offensive to the gospel. But the dulling of the mind leads to ultimate disorganization of the private world.

I understand premature success because I, too, discovered in my early thirties that I was coasting on natural talent and not giving adequate attention to the development of my mind. I began to see that unless I did something about it, my mind would not adequately serve me in later years when I wanted to be running at peak mental stride, doing and giving my very best.

For me, it meant that if I was going to become a more effective preacher, a more sensitive listener to struggling people, and a more useful leader, I would have to take seriously the challenge of sharpening my mental capacities so I could deal with my public world. Although I was not entirely asleep intellectually, I was not doing enough of the hard, disciplined work that would help me to be the innovative and seminal person I thought God wanted me to be.

No wonder I felt the pangs of disorganization when I faced situations in which I was not smart enough to understand what was going on. Like someone with a weight too heavy to lift, I found myself more and more trying to hoist ideas and perplexities that I was not mentally strong enough to get off the ground.

"The man of action has the present," wrote Oliver Wendell Holmes, "but the thinker controls the future."[3]

Although many so-called Christians have made an outspoken commitment to education with a Christian base, there has not always been a high enough value placed on the development of the mind. Few of us have fully appreciated the contrast between gatherers of details and rules and skilled handlers of truth. There may be some who know a little about a lot of things, but that does not guarantee that many of us know how to think deeply and insightfully about what we know.

I have been with men and women who have pressed enormous amounts of information about the Bible into their heads. They have learned to speak a rich vocabulary of correct Christian jargon. Their prayers can be so smooth-sounding that everyone listens in awe. We think them to be spiritual people. But at other times, we begin to see that they are rigid and inflexible, impervious to change and innovation. Their response to any serious challenge to their thought is a burst of anger or accusation.

Like many before me, I am convinced that Christians ought to be the strongest, broadest, most creative thinkers in the world. Again, it was Paul who said that as Christ-followers we are given the mind of Christ. This provides a potential intellectual breadth that the unregenerate mind does not possess. It offers an eternal, timeless perspective in which to think. In Christ there is a foundation of truth that ought to make our ideas, our analysis of things, and our innovations among the most powerful of the age. But because there is an essential laziness and internal disorganization in many Christian lives, this is not always the case. We are forfeiting one of the great gifts God provided through Christ.

For many years Admiral Hyman Rickover headed the United States Nuclear Navy. His admirers and his critics held strongly opposing views about the stern and demanding admiral. As long as he was in charge, every officer aboard a nuclear ship was personally interviewed and approved by Rickover. Those who went through those interviews usually came out shaking in fear, anger, or total intimidation. Among them was former president Jimmy Carter, who, years ago, applied for service under Rickover. This is his account of a Rickover interview:

I had applied for the nuclear submarine program, and Admiral Rickover was interviewing me for the job. It was the first time I met Admiral Rickover, and we sat in a large room by ourselves for more than two hours, and he let me choose any subjects I wished to discuss. Very carefully, I chose those about which I knew most at the time—current events, seamanship, music, literature, naval tactics, electronics, gunnery—and he began to ask me a series of questions of increasing difficulty. In each instance, he soon proved that I knew relatively little about the subject I had chosen.

He always looked right into my eyes, and he never smiled. I was saturated with cold sweat.

Finally, he asked a question and I thought I could redeem myself. He said, "How did you stand in your class at the Naval Academy?" Since I had completed my sophomore year at Georgia Tech before entering Annapolis as a plebe, I had done very well, and I swelled my chest with pride and answered, "Sir, I stood fifty-ninth in a class of 820!" I sat back to wait for the congratulations—which never came. Instead, the question: "Did you do your best?" I started to say, "Yes, sir," but I remembered who this was and recalled several of the many times at the Academy when I could have learned more about our allies, our enemies, weapons, strategy, and so forth. I was just human. I finally gulped and said, "No, sir, I didn't always do my best."

He looked at me for a long time, and then turned his chair around to end the interview. He asked one final question, which I have never been able to forget—or to answer. He said, "Why not?" I sat there for a while, shaken, and then slowly left the room.[4]

That encounter became the thought-starter for President Carter's book *Why Not the Best?* And it is a worthwhile story to ponder. Does not the man or woman who claims to walk with Christ owe the Creator excellence in terms of thought?

Thinking is the amazing capacity God has given the human being to discover and observe the stuff of creation, to compare and contrast each of its parts, and when possible, to use them properly so as to reflect the glory of the Creator. Thinkers see old things in new ways; they analyze hypotheses, separating out the true from the false. Thinkers sometimes describe old truths in new words and forms; they help others to see how applications to life can be made. Thinkers make bold decisions, help us see new visions, and overcome obstacles in previously unseen ways.

These are not merely the exercises of the great and the brilliant. They are the tasks of everyone with a healthy mind. As with physical bodies, some of us may be stronger than others, but that does not relieve us of the responsibility of using our bodies or our minds.

It would do us good to see ourselves as sponges. Throughout the expanse of creation God has hidden things for humankind to discover, to enjoy, and with which to perceive the nature of the Creator Himself. We should sponge it all up. Proverbs 25:2 says, "It is the glory of God to conceal a matter, / But the glory of kings is to search out a matter."

The work of the first man and woman was to discover and identify things God had made. Because of their disobedience against God's laws, some of the opportunity for that kind of marvelous work was forfeited. They now had to worry more about surviving in a hostile world than continuing to discover what was in it. The nature of work abruptly changed. I have a conviction that the heavenly life will in some way recover that original form of work.

But the principle and privilege of discovery still prevails in part. Some discoveries come through hard physical labor, such as digging gold out of the side of a hill. Other discoveries are made as we observe the progress of living things in the plant, animal, and human kingdoms. And much of the exploration of creation is done purely within the mind. We dig, as it were, and uncover ideas and truths; then we turn around to express them artistically, worshipfully, and inventively.

Thinking is a great work. It is best done with a mind that has trained and is in shape, just as competitive running is done with a body that has trained and is in shape. The best kind of thinking is accomplished when it is done in the context of reverence for God's kingly reign over all creation. It is sad to see great thinking and artistic work accomplished by men and women who have no interest in uncovering knowledge of the Creator. They think and innovate purely for self-aggrandizement or for the development of a human system that assumes it can get along without God.

Some Christians appear to be afraid to think. They mistake the gathering of facts, doctrinal systems, and lists of rules for thinking. They are uneasy when dealing with ambiguity. And they do not see the significance of wrestling with great ideas if they cannot always come up with easily packaged answers. The consequences are a drift toward mediocrity in personal living and mental activity and a loss of much that God meant for His children to enjoy as they walk through creation discovering His handiwork. Life under such circumstances becomes amusement, function without thought.

The unthinking Christ-follower does not realize it, but he is dangerously absorbed into the culture about him. Because his mind is untrained and unfilled, it lacks the ability to produce the hard questions with which the world needs to be challenged. The challenge for the modern Christ-follower in a secular society may be to *ask* prophetic questions before there is opportunity to provide Christ-oriented answers.

Sometimes, because of the massive amounts of information bombarding us regularly, the unthinking Christian longs to run in retreat, leaving heavy thinking up to a few elite Christian leaders or theologians.

In my lifetime I have watched the first decades of the Digital Revolution come to pass. I purchased one of the very first IBM PCs. So new was this wonderful innovation that the Sears and Roebuck salesman who sold it to me had no idea how to make it run.

Today, I am probably into my tenth computer, not counting laptops, tablets, and iPads. I have learned how to use Word, Excel, PowerPoint, Filemaker, and a host of apps.

Most of the time I love this world of technology, and I am continuously thankful for the way it has served my interests.

But I also have come to realize how it affects one's mind, one's soul. Newer generations have embraced what I have chosen to avoid: social networking, which too often cheapens the art of conversation, destroys people through electronic gossip, and oversaturates us with a Niagara of information.

I could never be a Luddite, and I admit to impatience in conversations where people simply want to knock technology without sorting the benefits from the liabilities. I love being able to Skype with Gail when we are on two different continents. I have appreciated the convenience of iMessaging when there's a need to get a fast message to a colleague or a friend. Being a bit of a writer, I can't say enough about how much better it is to delete paragraphs rather than shove new pieces of paper into a typewriter.

But this I do know. The follower of Jesus must be perceptive in knowing when technology becomes an obstacle to the growing of one's faith. Not an easy thing to discern.

When the Christian's mind becomes dull, he can fall prey to the propaganda of a non-Christian scheme of things, led by people who have not neglected their thinking powers—and have simply outthought us.

Just as my coach once taught me to train my body so I could finish the race, so I had to learn what others are having to learn: the mind also must be trained. The private world of a Christ-follower will be weak, defenseless, and disorganized if serious attention has not been given to this sector of intellectual growth.

The man from Poly Prep was a better runner, but he lost. He lost because 100 yards of talent is not good enough for 440 yards of race.

When I once evaluated the order of the intellectual sector of my private world, I thankfully came to see that a few natural gifts or a few years of education were never going to make me the man God wanted to use in any part of the world where He wanted me to do work. If I was going to endure and become useful to the level of my potential, it would not be because I was talented or degreed but because I had learned to take the muscles of my mind and work them into shape.

I had to become a thinker. I had to become conversant with the directions that history was taking. I needed to know how to grapple with the great ideas of humankind. And I had to learn how to make independent judgments about what I was seeing. It was time for me to start working—hard. Other runners were catching up, and the race was far from over. I didn't want to be a better man in the first turn and a loser at the finish line because I had talent but no endurance.

In his journal, Oswald Chambers wrote:

A great fear has been at work in my mind and God has used it to arouse me to prayer. I came across a man whom I knew years ago, a mighty man of God, and now ten years have gone and I meet him again—*garrulous and unenlivened* [shallow and superficial]. How many men seem to become like that after forty years of age! The fear of sloth and indulgence has come home with a huge fear and fairly driven me to God to keep me from ever forgetting what I owe him.[5]

Apparently, Chambers was greatly marked by this encounter of which he wrote because he reflected on it again sometime later: "I hate to meet a man whom I have met ten years ago and find that he is at precisely the same point, neither moderated nor quickened nor experienced but simply stiffened."

Think about it!

NINE

THE SADNESS OF A BOOK NEVER READ

GAIL AND I WERE BROWSING IN AN OLD BOOKSTORE ONE DAY LOOKING for those special titles among secondhand books that are such a delight when found. Gail found a copy of a biography of Daniel Webster that had been published in the 1840s. It looked interesting, and since we are lovers of biographies, she purchased the book.

The cover of the book appeared worn enough to convey the notion that it had been well read. One could imagine that it had been a prized edition in the library of several generations of a New England family. Perhaps it had been loaned out on several occasions and brought enlightenment to a dozen different readers.

Not so! When Gail began to leaf through the old book, she discovered that the printer had failed to properly cut the pages, and many of them could not be opened until one took a blade and cut them apart. The uncut pages were clear evidence that the book had never been read! It looked on the outside as if it had been constantly used. But if it had, it was only in gracing a library shelf, playing doorstop, or providing height to a small child so he could sit and reach the table while he ate. The book may have been used, but it certainly had never been read.

The Christian who is not growing intellectually is like a book whose many pages remain unopened and unread. Like the book, he may be of some value, but not nearly as much as if he had chosen to sharpen and develop his mind.

As a body grows flabby when it is not exposed to physical labor or challenging exercise, so the mind weakens, gets out of shape, when it is not given proper training. I'd never given much thought to *thinking* as a discipline until I read an old book (1928) by a French writer, Ernest Dimnet, called *The Art of Thinking*. I love these lines of his. When you read them, remember . . . they are almost ninety years old.

> Enter Thinker. We have all seen him standing amidst the surprised, incredulous and often silly group of non-thinkers. Sometimes he is a very simple man, the roadside mechanic slowly walking out of his garage. Round the car two or three men, hot with ineffective guessing, are still talking excitedly when the taciturn man appears; for an hour they have talked, tried and failed. They stop and not another word is heard. The intelligent eyes of the artisan, helped by his seeming infallible hands, go over the organs of the machine; meanwhile we know that his mind is going over dozens of hypotheses which to us are only riddles. Soon the trouble is found. Sometimes the man smiles. At what? At whom? I often wonder. At any rate we have felt the presence of a brain.

Dimnet has other examples, but I love this one best of all. How clever! A mechanic as a thinker. I would never have thought of it as an example. But it is wonderful. And I can picture all the other know-it-alls standing around, quiet in their incredulity. "We have felt the presence of a brain," he said. No harm reading a masterful sentence twice.

Dimnet later wrote:

THE SADNESS OF A BOOK NEVER READ

The thinker . . . is preeminently a [person] who sees where others do not. The novelty of what he says, its character as a sort of revelation, the charm that attaches to it, all come from the fact that he sees. He seems to be head and shoulders above the crowd, or to be walking on the ridge-way while others trudge at the bottom. Independence is the word which describes the moral aspect of this capacity for vision.[1]

In his best days, this was what Solomon must have been. A man who looked into things seeking meaning. One who could put ideas together and come up with sensible conclusions. One who loved the stuff of creation and wasn't afraid to search out the knowledge of it.

[Solomon] spoke three thousand proverbs and his songs numbered a thousand and five. He spoke about plant life, from the cedar of Lebanon to the hyssop that grows out of walls. He also spoke about animals and birds, reptiles and fish. From all nations people came to listen to Solomon's wisdom. (1 Kings 4:32–34 NIV)

How do we encourage the development of people like this? People of substance who speak thoughtfully. Who do not capitulate to shallow ideas. Who are not intellectually lazy, living under the dominance of other, more strident minds. Who are able to search the nooks and crannies of possibilities and summon deep judgment. Who are not captive to ideologies that leave no room for independent conclusions or actions.

PUTTING YOURSELF IN A GROWTH MODE

When a person sets out to deliberately use his mind for the purpose of growth and development as a person, new order comes into his private world. His mind—an organ largely undeveloped in many people—comes alive with new possibility when he sets himself in what I call a *growth mode*.

There are at least three objectives in developing the intellectual dimension of our private worlds. Let me offer them to you as a scheme for mental development.

1. THE MIND MUST BE DISCIPLINED TO THINK CHRISTIANLY. I understand this objective because I grew up in a Christian context and had the full advantage of Christian teaching from infancy.

To think Christianly means to look at our world from the perspective that it is made and owned by God, that what we do with creation will have to be accounted for, and that it is important to make choices according to the laws of God. The Bible calls this *stewardship*. Christian thinking looks at all issues and ideas from the standpoint of what God desires and what might give honor to Him.

A person who has not enjoyed the advantage of a lifelong Christian context is not liable to gain that total perspective easily. If he becomes a follower of Christ at a later age, it will be particularly bothersome to compare his instincts and reactions to those of more mature believers. He will tend to be hard on himself, wondering if he will ever get ahead in matters of faith.

For this kind of person, thinking will be done more by *commitment* than by *Christian instinct*. In other words, the newer Christ-follower's reaction to a problem or opportunity is apt to be a non-Christian one, and he will then have to reverse and replace it with a learned Christian response.

The person who thinks Christianly by background probably thinks with all the proper reactions unless he deliberately chooses to embrace a life of rebellion. But—and this is important—whether he follows up the Christian mental response with Christian action is another matter. The mental response without the action is of little use.

I describe these two styles of thought because I have found it to be helpful to people, especially younger Christ-followers who are struggling with the meaning of spiritual growth. They wonder why they are always just a second behind older believers and seem unable to catch up. The key is often in Christian acculturation, which is certainly an advantage and testifies to the importance of the Christian family. This kind of Christian acculturation is becoming less and less frequent as the world around us grows increasingly secular and drifts from a Christian base.

For the new Christ-follower, mental growth will be in part the cultivation of the Christian perspective, the Christian response to life, and the Christian value system in the marketplace.

The long-term believer has a struggle of a different sort. Although he may have an instinctive Christian reaction to most situations, his commitment may not be as enthusiastic as the newly converted believer. He simply assumes that Christianized mechanisms will work automatically. And this can be very dangerous over a period of time. Thinking Christianly without a regular renewal of our commitment to Christ leads to a deadness of religion, a boring faith, an ineffective witness to God. And we who have grown up with the gospel of Christ have to be very careful to avoid this.

2. THE MIND MUST BE TAUGHT TO OBSERVE AND APPRECIATE THE MESSAGES GOD HAS WRITTEN IN CREATION. "The heavens are telling of the glory of God" (Ps. 19:1). Everything God made— even human beings—has as its key purpose the reflection of the honor of God.

Unfortunately, the power of sin has tarnished the capacity of some aspects of creation to reflect that honor. In fact, sin first appears to have done its job on humanity; then, through men and women, sin systematically trashed everything else in creation. But where man has not been able to confuse the issue, the creation continues to shout out its message: God the Creator be praised!

The growing mind, filled with the love of Christ, searches creation for these messages. Because of our spiritual and natural gifts, each of us is able to see and hear them in particular areas more than in others. And we are enabled to take this creation material and identify it, shape it, reconfigure it, or in other ways use it so that God is further glorified. The carpenter works with wood; the physician listens to the body; the musician arranges sounds; the executive manages people; the educator trains students; the researcher analyzes, innovates, and implements with the elements of the universe.

We develop our minds for these tasks, and we rejoice as we do them for all that God is revealing to us out of His loving heart.

3. THE MIND MUST BE TRAINED TO PURSUE INFORMATION, IDEAS, AND INSIGHTS FOR THE PURPOSE OF SERVING THE PEOPLE OF THE PUBLIC WORLD. The development of the mind makes it possible for men and women to be servants to the generation in which they live. I think of the contributions of missionary-physician Paul Brand, who is credited with the development of surgical procedures that have restored the use of limbs to those suffering from Hansen's disease (leprosy). We have all been enriched by the mind of C. S. Lewis in literature or Dr. Martin Luther King Jr. in race relations. And there are men and women whose names are not as well known: a young civil engineer who uses his expertise to help build a hydroelectric dam in Ecuador; an accountant who gives precious time to help disadvantaged people restructure themselves financially; a builder who goes into the inner city and teaches men and women to rehabilitate and winterize old houses; and a computer operator who gives time to teach immigrant children to read. All of these are using their minds in ministry to others.

We do not develop our intellects merely for our own personal advancement, but we put our thinking power to work for the use of others. I remember this when I push myself in my reading and filing: I am collecting the raw material that will become a sermon or book of encouragement or insight for others one day. As my mind grows, it may make possible the growth of others.

ORGANIZING THE MIND TO MAKE IT GROW

Looking back across the early years of my life, I recall once coming to the startling realization that although I had amassed enormous amounts of information about many things, I had never really pushed myself to be an aggressive thinker. In fact, I am not sure I had ever learned to love learning.

My father was a strong and dominating thinker. It was as if he did the family's thinking for us. To express a thought contrary to his when I was a boy was no simple matter, and I often lost the courage to do so. My problem! So when I "graduated" from my family of origin, I had some catching up to do in the area of original thinking. And I often wonder if I have ever caught up.

Moving through my educational years, I tended to be one of those who played the margins. "Tell me what it takes to pass this course," I said, "and I'll give it to you." With rare exceptions, I adopted that philosophy throughout high school, college, and graduate school. Occasionally I would be confronted by an instructor who saw through that limited view and would push me toward a higher excellence. I never stopped to ask myself why I appreciated those instructors more than the others. It was indeed fun to be stretched, to have something better than the average pulled out of me.

But when I finally left the formal education process behind, there was no one to push or pull me, no one to require intellectual excellence except myself. And soon I learned that I would have to accept full responsibility for my own mental growth. That was when I achieved intellectual puberty. For the first time, I became serious about learning how to think and learn on my own.

How does one go about this process of intellectual organization in the private world? Let me suggest several ways:

We Grow by Becoming Listeners

My intellectual organization began when I learned to listen. For someone like me who enjoys talking, listening can be a challenge. But if a person is not a listener, he denies his mind a major source of information by which to grow.

Perhaps the first step in becoming a listener is to *learn to ask questions*. I have rarely met a person or been in a situation where there was not something valuable worth learning. On many occasions, I have had to generate listening by first asking questions. That has meant learning how to be a good question asker. Right questions elicit valuable information for the purposes of growth. I like to ask men and women about their jobs, where they met their spouses, what they have been reading about, what they consider their greatest present challenges, and where they find God most alive in their lives. The answers are always useful.

In the process of becoming a listener, I have come to see that most people are eager to share something of themselves. Many older people rarely have anyone to listen to them, and they are usually wellsprings of insight. Suffering people, people under stress and tension, have much to share with those who can learn to ask the right questions. And in asking we not only learn, but we are also able to encourage and love.

We particularly need to learn to listen to older people and children. They all have stories to tell that enrich the mind and the heart. Children simplify things, often with brutal honesty. Older people bring the perspective of their long years on issues. Suffering people also help us understand what are the truly important matters of life. There is something to learn from all people if we are only willing to sit at their feet and humble ourselves enough to ask the right questions.

A second way of growing through listening comes when we *listen to mentors.* Throughout my life God has surrounded me with a chain of men and women who believed in me, cared for me, and tried to make a contribution to the bringing forth of whatever potential God had placed in me. I am grateful that I was taught by my parents to listen to such people, for many of my colleagues tended to slough off the counsel and wisdom of such mentors and so lost valuable information.

Third, I can suggest that growth always comes when we also *listen to our critics.* And that is not an easy thing for any of us to do. Dawson Trotman, the founder of the Navigators, had a good method for handling all criticisms directed at himself. No matter how unfair the criticism might seem to be, he would always take it into his prayer closet and, in effect, spread it before the Lord. Then he would say, "Lord, please show me the kernel of truth hidden in this criticism."

The truth may certainly be small on occasion, but it is always worth finding and thinking through. I have been grateful to learn of Dawson Trotman's secret. It has saved me countless bad moments when I might have otherwise been tempted to be defensive when criticized. Instead I began to learn to grow at the hands of my critics. I have seldom ever heard a criticism about myself that didn't indeed contain a kernel of useful truth. Some of the kernels have been on the small side, but they were there.

When I mentally list the most important truths on which I have based my own character and personality development, I am astonished to discover that a large majority of them came through painful situations where someone, either out of love or anger, rebuked or criticized me soundly. I carry with me the memory of a time when my missiology professor at Denver Seminary, Dr. Raymond Buker, approached me at the end of a special convocation, wherein I had read a paper on some moral issue that was burning in the hearts of the student generation of that time. I had cut two of his classes that day to prepare the paper, and it had not gone unnoticed.

"Gordon," he said, "the paper you read tonight was a good one, but it wasn't a great one. Would you like to know why?"

I wasn't sure I really wanted to know because I anticipated a bit of humiliation coming my way, but I swallowed hard and told Dr. Buker that I would like to hear his analysis.

"The paper wasn't a great one," he said as he thumped his finger on my chest, "because you sacrificed the routine to write it."

In pain I learned one of the most important lessons I ever needed to learn. Because my time as a Christian leader has been generally my own to use as I please, it would be very easy to avoid routine, unspectacular duties, and give myself only to the exciting things that come along. But most of life is lived in the routine, and Buker was right: the man or woman who learns to make peace with routine responsibilities and obligations will make the greatest contributions in the long run.

But I would not have learned that lesson and grown from it, at least at that point in my life, if there had not been a man willing to rebuke me and if I had not been willing to listen and learn.

We grow through listening, aggressive listening: asking questions, watching intently what is happening around us, taking note of the good or ill consequences that befall people as a result of their choice making.

We Grow Through Reading

A second way we grow is through reading. In our age of mass media, the younger generation is finding it harder and harder to

acquire the discipline of reading, and that may be one of the greatest losses of our time. Nothing substitutes for what can be found
when we embrace the world of books.

The Roman philosopher Cicero said of the discipline of reading:

> No other pleasure suits every occasion, every age or every place.
> But the study of letters is the food of youth, the delight of old
> age, a delight at home and no burden abroad; it stays with us at
> night, and goes with us on our travels, near and far.

Paul gave evidence of his own hunger for reading when he wrote
to Timothy asking for parchments and books. Even at that older
age, he was anxious to grow. Some of us are not naturally given to
reading, and it is hard for us. But to whatever extent we can press
ourselves in this direction, we should acquire the habit of reading
systematically.

My wife, Gail, and I are avid readers of biography, and there is
hardly a time in our home when the two of us are not making our
way through one biography or another. These books have poured
priceless insights into our minds.

Others will be drawn to psychology, theology, history, or good
fiction. But all of us need to have at least one good book going
at all times, more if possible. When I visit with pastors who are
struggling with their own effectiveness, I often ask, "What are you
reading lately?" It is almost predictable that if a pastor is struggling
with failure in his ministry, he will be unable to name a title or an
author that he has been reading in recent days. If he is not reading, the chances are strong that he is not growing. And if he is not
growing, then he may rapidly slip into ineffectiveness.

It seems like a century since America struggled through the
hostage crisis in Iran (1979–1981). Those of us who remember that

ordeal will not forget one woman who seemed to stand out from the other fifty or more victims who were held for more than four hundred days. Kathryn Koob became an inspiration to many in the embassy and here in the United States. When she returned to her home and was able to describe what kept her both sane and strong while in such conditions, she readily acknowledged that it was the reading and memorizing she had done throughout her life. In her mind was stored an almost infinite amount of material from which she drew strength and resolve as well as the truth with which to comfort others.

In my own disciplines, I have tried to set aside a minimum of an hour each day for the purpose of reading. I have found that one should never read without a pencil in hand to mark salient passages, and I have developed a simple series of codes that will remind me of impressive thoughts or quotes worth clipping and filing for future use.

As I read, I jot down key thoughts and ideas, which become the grist for sermons or articles. Not infrequently an insight jumps out that can be of value to someone I know. It has often been a form of ministry to make a copy of that particular quote or reference and send it along as a piece of encouragement or instruction.

If an author has been particularly stimulating to my mind and heart, I will attempt to acquire everything he or she has written. And I will take careful note of bibliographies, footnotes, and indexes for material worth checking into myself.

Over the years, I have learned to ask anyone I know to be a student or reader of any kind, "What are you reading?" If the person can suggest a half-dozen titles, I am most grateful and put them on a reading list. You can always tell the readers in a group when someone mentions a particularly excellent book. The readers are the ones who immediately take out a notebook or reference card and jot down the name and author.

We Grow Through Purposeful Study

A third way to grow mentally is through the discipline of study. The amount of time spent studying will vary for all of us and will have a lot to do with our vocations. Preachers simply have to study if they are going to provide the sort of pulpit "feeding" that they have been mandated to do.

In my earliest years of ministry, when this business of mental growth had not yet become a discipline for me, most of my study was what I now call *defensive study*. By that I mean that I studied frantically simply because I had an upcoming sermon to preach or talk to give. And all my study was centered on the completion of that task.

But later I discovered the importance of something I now call *offensive study*. This is study that has as its objective the gathering of large clusters of information and insight out of which future sermons and talks, books, and articles may grow. In the former kind of study, one is restricted to one chosen subject. In the latter, one is exploring, turning up truth and understanding from scores of sources. Both forms of study, offensive and defensive, are necessary in my life.

We grow when we pursue the discipline of offensive study. This is done through reading, taking occasional courses that stretch our minds, taking on challenges that force us to learn new things, and exploring various disciplines for the sheer joy of learning more about God's world.

I found that summer was an ideal time for great offensive study; winter was not. Each year I set aside certain books and projects with which I wished to acquaint myself, and when the summer months provided extra space, I got busy. I hoped that by the end of the summer, I would be ready to move into the heavier months of the year with considerable amounts of raw material in my notebooks for sermons and Bible studies throughout the coming church year.

As I mentioned earlier in this book, my own study time has

always been best accomplished in the early morning hours. But in the past I was able to achieve it only because I'd budgeted space for it in the calendar far in advance of the date. When I cheated on the time, I almost always ended up regretting it. Studying was a date in the calendar that should never have been broken.

I have always enjoyed the support of a wife who protected and encouraged my study time, and that was a part of her growth as well. In our early years of marriage and ministry, she had to learn the importance of offensive and defensive study just as I had to. As a young wife, when she saw me reading a book or sitting at my desk, she didn't hesitate to interrupt me. After all, it was easy to surmise, what is a thirty-second interruption for a question or a quick break to take out the garbage?

But Gail came to see that study is hard work for me and that interruptions often shatter mental momentum. With that realization, she not only became a protector of my time but a creator of it, skillfully admonishing me if she caught me wasting any of it or procrastinating on my commitments. None of my books would ever have been written if she had not determined with me that my writing was part of the call of God on my life and I would need her support as well as her prodding.

A while ago I led a seminar for pastors on the subject of preaching and discussed the matters of study and preparation. Since a number of spouses (male and female both) were present when I spoke, I said to the group, "Now, some of you may be tempted to think that when your spouse is reading, they are really wasting time. So you may feel free to interrupt them on impulse. What you need to realize is that they are working every bit as much as the carpenter who is in his shop sharpening the blade of a saw. Within reason, you ought not only to avoid interrupting your spouses, but also to try your best to maximize their privacy if you want them to grow in effectiveness."

Studying means developing good filing systems to store my information so that it is never wasted. It means making sacrifices to acquire a good library of reference books. But most of all, it means determination and discipline. And the result is always growth.

One more comment about the importance of studying for all of us. I have talked primarily about pastors because that has been my world and because study is so important to leaders. But I am speaking in principle to all Christ-followers, to all men and women. I have realized the importance not only of my wife's making it possible for me to study but also of my making it possible for her to study. This is a mutual discipline to which we encourage each other—both of us should be engaging in growth of the mind.

I want to make clear that this means that *we who are husbands need to ask whether we are creating and guarding time for our spouses to read and study.* We have been startled by the number of couples we have met whose problem is uneven intellectual growth. After ten or fifteen years of marital relationship, one is growing while the other is not. Too often, the one who is growing the most is the *woman.* Can I be blunt? Too many men seem to stop growing intellectually when they reach their midforties.

You can recognize students of every age primarily because they tend to be note takers. Many years ago Gail and I adopted a special-size notebook paper and bought dozens of loose-leaf binders. All of our notes go into those books under special topical codes. We go virtually nowhere without paper so that we are ready to record the thoughts of someone who might come across our path and have something significant to say. One never knows when he or she will turn up a book or come upon an experience worth recording for future reference.

The Christ-follower who wants to grow will always take notes when sermons are being preached or Bible classes are being taught. It is one practical way of asserting faith that God is going to give the listener something that will be useful in the future in the service of others. Good note taking is one way to store the information and insights that are constantly coming at us, and therefore to take advantage of all the possible growth that is available to us.

The Old Testament scribe Ezra believed in the growth of the mind. "For Ezra had set his heart to study the law of the LORD and to practice it, and to teach His statutes and ordinances in Israel" (7:10). The order of this description of personal growth in a man's private world is worth noting: *He studied; he did what he learned; he shared what was worthwhile.* Ezra was a professional student of sorts, putting in far more time than any of us will ever do. But he set a great precedent. And because his mind and spirit were full, God tapped Ezra for the gigantic task of leading a large task force of men across the wilderness to rebuild Jerusalem.

If you were to come to our home today and take that old Webster biography off the shelf, you would discover that we have slit open every page so that we could read the story of that fascinating American life. The book still looks terribly worn, but now it is worn for the right reason: it has finally been read!

Like the book, when we found it, many people show the outer marks of the wear and tear of life. But inside, large areas of their private world remain unopened. They are disorganized within because they have never stretched and conditioned their minds to handle the information and challenges of the age. They have not taken advantage of all that God has placed here for us to discover, enjoy, and use.

But when we take seriously the growth and development of our minds, a beautiful thing happens. We come to know God more fully, and we are infinitely more useful in the service of others, for in just the way that creation was originally designed, we—our sharpened minds—begin to reflect the glory of God also.

What a beautiful thing to see: a human being in God's world with a sharpened mind, having opened every page with insight and truth. "Hold on to instruction," the book of Proverbs says, and "do not let it go; / guard it well, for it is your life" (4:13 NIV).

TEN

ORDER IN THE GARDEN

HOWARD RUTLEDGE, A UNITED STATES AIR FORCE PILOT, WAS SHOT down over North Vietnam during the early stages of the war. He spent several miserable years in the hands of his captors before being released at the war's conclusion.

I have Rutledge's book, *In the Presence of Mine Enemies*, in my library. Though many years old, it is a favorite. I appreciate Rutledge's openness in describing the inner resources (or lack of them) from which he drew in those arduous days when life seemed so intolerable.

> During those longer periods of enforced reflection it became so much easier to separate the important from the trivial, the worthwhile from the waste. For example, in the past, I usually worked or played hard on Sundays and had no time for church. For years Phyllis [his wife] had encouraged me to join the family at church. She never nagged or scolded—she just kept hoping. But I was too busy, too preoccupied, to spend one or two short hours a week thinking about the really important things.

Now the sights and sounds and smells of death were all around me. My hunger for spiritual food soon outdid my hunger for a steak. Now I wanted to know about that part of me that will never die. Now I wanted to talk about God and Christ and the church. But in Heartbreak [the name POWS gave their prison camp] solitary confinement, there was no pastor, no Sunday-School teacher, no Bible, no hymnbook, no community of believers to guide and sustain me.

I had completely neglected the spiritual dimension of my life. It took prison to show me how empty life is without God.[1]

It took the pressure of a POW camp to show Rutledge that there was a center to his private world that he had been neglecting virtually all of his life. I like to refer to this center as a person's spirit; others call it the soul. You can't physiologically locate the spiritual center of a person's private world, but it is there. It is eternal, and it is the point at which we most intimately commune with our heavenly Father. The spirit can never lose its eternal nature, but it can exist in a state of such disorganization that almost no communion with God is possible. That usually leads to a general chaos in other parts of one's private world.

I like Wallace Hamilton's way of describing the natural state of a person's interior life: "Within each of us there is a herd of wild horses all wanting to run loose."

The Christ-follower is convinced of the existence of the soul. But many Christians struggle with the quality of life within that center. At least, that is the impression I get when I listen for very long to those who are willing to talk about the meaning of private spiritual activity. Many men and women are painfully dissatisfied with their level of contact with God. "I just don't feel like I get through to Him very often," is a typical comment.

A disorganized spirit often means lack of inner serenity. For some, what should be tranquility is, in fact, only numbness or emptiness. Some suffer from restlessness, a feeling that they never quite measure up to the expectations they think God has for them. A common concern is the inability to maintain spiritual momentum, to have reasonably consistent attitudes and desires. "I start out my week with great intentions," a young person comments, "but by Wednesday morning, I've lost interest. I just can't sustain a spiritual life that is satisfying. So I get to the point where I'm tired of trying."

THE QUICK FIX

A look at the great saints of Scripture sometimes makes us envious. We reflect on the burning-bush experience of Moses, Isaiah's vision in the temple, and the confrontation Paul had on the road to Damascus. Those were powerful starts to noble lives of spiritual vitality.

We are tempted to say, "If I could have had an experience like any of those, I'd be spiritually fixed for life." We assume our spirituality might be enhanced by some dramatic moment that would indelibly burn itself upon our consciousness. Were we to be impressed by such a spectacular touch with God, we would never—so we think—be tempted to doubt the matter again.

That is one reason many of us are tempted to reach out for a sort of "quick fix" that makes God seem real and more intimate. Some feel deeply enriched if they are caused to feel terribly guilty by a preacher who angrily thunders forth with accusations and denunciations. Others quest after emotional experiences that lift them out of themselves into ecstatic levels. Sometimes one looks about in a so-called contemporary worship service and wonders what is really happening as people get caught up in the rhythmic, unbelievably loud, repetitive music. Is it worship, or is it a hypnotic experience that simply helps one forget the difficulties or the routines of real life outside the building?

There are those who immerse themselves in endless rounds of Bible teaching and study, making the search for pure doctrine a way of finding satisfactory intimacy with God. Still others pursue spirituality through busyness in the church. Usually our choice of these or other ways of filling the seemingly empty spirit is based on our psychological temperament—what most effectively touches us for the moment and makes us feel at peace.

But the fact is that the average person—like you and me—is not likely to have a great biblical confrontation; nor would we be satisfied by the dramatic experiences that happen to others. If we are ever to develop a spiritual life that gives contentment, it will be because we approach spiritual living as a discipline, much as the athlete trains his or her body for competition.

One thing is certain: if we do not choose to take on that discipline, there is the possibility of a day—as one came to Howard Rutledge—when we will regret that we had not undertaken the challenge.

CULTIVATING THE GARDEN

How shall we describe this center, this inner spiritual territory where encounters are almost too sacred for words? Beyond theological propositions, we are forced to speak through a collection of metaphors.

David of the Psalms was thinking in metaphors when he imagined his inner spirit to be like a pasture where God, the Shepherd, led him as a lamb. In his metaphor, he longed for calm waters, green pastures, and tables loaded with food to be eaten in safety. This was a place, David fantasized, where the soul was restored.

The eighteenth-century Christian poet William Cowper used the metaphor of a quiet pool:

> A life all turbulence and noise may seem
> To him that leads it wise and to be praised,
> But wisdom is a pearl with most success
> Sought in still waters. (from "The Task," book 3)

For me, the helpful metaphor for the inner spiritual center has been a garden, a place of potent peace and tranquility. This garden is a place where the Spirit of God comes to make self-disclosure, to share wisdom, to give affirmation or rebuke, to provide encouragement, and to give direction and guidance. When this garden is in proper order, it is a quiet place, and there is an absence of busyness, of defiling noise, of confusion.

The inner garden is a delicate place, and if not properly maintained it will be quickly overrun by intrusive undergrowth. God does not often walk in disordered gardens. And that is why inner gardens that are ignored are said to be empty.

That is exactly what Howard Rutledge was struggling with when the pressure was at its highest in "Heartbreak" prison. Total isolation, frequent beatings, and deteriorating health had made his world a hostile place. What resources did he have to draw on that would sustain him? According to his own admission, he'd squandered opportunities earlier in life to store up strength and resolve in his inner garden. "I was too busy, too preoccupied," he says, "to spend one or two short hours a week thinking about the really important things." Nevertheless, what little he had from his childhood, he seized and developed. Suddenly, God was a very real and very important part of his existence.

Bringing order to the spiritual dimension of our private worlds is spiritual gardening. It is the careful cultivation of spiritual ground. The gardener turns up soil, pulls out unwanted growth, plans the use of the ground, plants seeds, waters and nourishes, and enjoys the harvests that result. All of this is what many have called spiritual discipline.

I love the words of Brother Lawrence, a reflective Christian of many centuries ago, who used the metaphor of a chapel:

> It is not needful always to be in church to be with God. We make a chapel of our heart, to which we can from time to time withdraw to have gentle, humble, loving communion with Him. Everyone is able to have these familiar conversations with God. Some more, some less—He knows our capabilities. *Let us make a start. Perhaps He only waits for us to make one whole-hearted resolve.* Courage! We have but a short time to live.[2]

Let us begin soon, Brother Lawrence coaxes us; time is short! The discipline of the spirit must begin now.

WHAT WILL IT TAKE?

When the inner garden is under cultivation and God's Spirit is present, harvests are regular events. The fruits? Things like courage, hope, love, endurance, joy, and lots of peace. Unusual capacities for self-control and the ability to discern evil and to ferret out truth are also reaped. As the writer of the Proverbs put it,

> For wisdom will enter your heart
> And knowledge will be pleasant to your soul;
> Discretion will guard you,
> Understanding will watch over you,
> To deliver you from the way of evil,
> From the man who speaks perverse things. (2:10–12)

Richard Foster quotes a favorite author of mine, Thomas Kelly:

> We feel honestly the pull of many obligations and try to fulfill them all. And we are unhappy, uneasy, strained, oppressed, and fearful we shall be shallow. . . . We have hints that there is a way of life vastly richer and deeper than all this hurried existence, a life of unhurried serenity and peace and power. If only we could slip over into that Center! . . . We have seen and known some people who have found this deep Center of living, where the fretful calls of life are integrated, where No as well as Yes can be said with confidence.[3]

Kelly speaks to the point: if only we could slip over into that Center!

Down through the centuries the Christian mystics were the ones who took spiritual discipline most seriously. They studied it, practiced it, and not infrequently—we can't ignore this—carried the disciplines to unhealthy and dangerous extremes. But they believed that there had to be regular experiences of withdrawal from routines and relationships to seek God in an inner garden. They were quick to tell us that church services and religious celebrations were far from adequate. A man or a woman had to develop a chapel, still waters, or a garden in the private world, they said. There was no alternative.

Jesus certainly pursued the discipline of His spirit. We know that David did. And so did Moses, the apostles, and Paul, who wrote of his own routines:

> I run in such a way, as not without aim; I box in such a way, as not beating the air; but I discipline my body and make it my slave, so that, after I have preached to others, I myself will not be disqualified. (1 Cor. 9:26–27)

Have we cheapened this spiritual discipline, this cultivation of the inner garden? Christ-followers today talk about the importance of "quiet time," a daily devotional often reduced to a system or method that is swift and streamlined. We boil it down to seven minutes or thirty minutes, depending on how much time we have available. We use Bible study guides, devotional guides, devotional booklets, and carefully organized prayer lists, all of which are nice—better, I suppose, than nothing—but not nearly as effective as what the mystics had in mind.

A major Christian magazine once called me to ask if I would spend a day with an outstanding Christian leader from another country who was visiting our city of Boston. They wanted me to lead him through an in-depth interview about himself so readers could gain insight into him as a person. I called on him to request permission for the conversation.

"And what shall we talk about?" he asked me.

"I thought we'd talk about your life as a preacher, a writer, and a scholar," I said. "Perhaps we could get into your views of family life, friendships, and your spiritual disciplines—"

"My spiritual disciplines?" he broke in.

"Yes," I came back. "A lot of people would love to know something of the ways in which you've pursued a personal walk with God."

I'll never forget his response.

"That part of my life is far too private to share with anyone."

I still think that many of us who are younger men and women in ministry would have profited from this older man's insights; nevertheless, I heard what he was trying to say. That part of his private world was just that: *strictly private*. It had been developed in a kind of secrecy, and it would stay that way. He and God would share it together—and alone. It would not be reduced to a system so that it could be adopted or imported into someone else's experience.

I have thought often about this man's reluctance to open

his personal life at the depth I wished to explore. Perhaps it was because he was of another culture that he did not understand our American curiosity and our tendency to blab about everything that is personal to us, even if it risks uncovering too much of ourselves. One does wonder if we have simply talked too much in our books and magazine articles—told one another too much when we should have reserved the conversation for God alone. Just a thought. At least one I need to think.

What will it take to force us into disciplined cultivation of the inner garden of our private worlds? Will it require an experience of severe suffering? That is what history seems to say over and over again: those under pressure seek God because there is nothing else. Those smothered in "blessings" tend to drift with the current. And that is why I question the word *blessing* sometimes. Surely something is not a blessing if it seduces us away from inward spiritual cultivation.

Can the importance of the inward center ever be appreciated until we have come close to death, defeat, or humiliation? But the command and the precedents come to us over and over again, in the Scriptures and through the history of the great saints. He who orders his inner spiritual world will make a place for God to visit and speak. And when that voice is heard, it will be unlike anything else ever spoken. That is what Howard Rutledge discovered. But it took a prisoner-of-war experience to force him to find it out.

Brother Lawrence says, "Let us make a start." Thomas Kelly admonishes: "Slip over into that Center!" Jesus calls, "Come learn of Me." How does this discipline of the spirit happen?

ELEVEN

NO OUTER PROPS NECESSARY

WHEN E. STANLEY JONES, METHODIST MISSIONARY TO INDIA, WAS AN aged man, he had a debilitating stroke that left him immobile and virtually speechless. But not faithless. "I need no outer props to hold up my faith," he wrote, "for my faith holds me." But he sadly saw that his was not the experience of everyone around him.

> I was talking to a bishop who had retired. He was frustrated. When he was no longer in the limelight of the bishopric, he was frustrated and told me so. He wanted to know the secret of victorious living. I told him it was in self-surrender. *The difference was in giving up the innermost self to Jesus.* The difference was in the texture of the things that held him. When the outer strands were broken by retirement, the inner strands were not enough to hold him. Apparently he had a case of "limelight-itis" instead of a case of surrender to Jesus.
>
> *Fortunately, with me, surrender to Jesus was the primary thing, and when the outer strands were cut by this stroke, my life didn't shake.*[1]

Jones understood what Thomas Kelly is saying when he calls for us to slip over into the center. Who of us would not like to have Jones's perspective and endurance? But how many of us are destined, due to neglect of our inner garden, to fall into the trap the bishop set for himself? How do we cultivate the inner garden of our private worlds?

Because this book is not primarily a treatment of spiritual disciplines, I cannot survey all the ways the saints have found to strengthen the inner spirit. Instead, I have selected five spiritual exercises of critical importance—the last two of which are discussed in the next two chapters—exercises that I find many Christ followers neglecting. They are: the pursuit of *silence and solitude*; *singing*; regularly *listening to God*; the experience of *reflection and meditation*; and *prayer as worship and intercession*.

SILENCE AND SOLITUDE

The desert fathers of centuries ago, Henri Nouwen tells us, understood the importance of a silent environment for the cultivation of the spirit when they called out to one another, *"Fuge, terche, et quisset"*—silence, solitude, and inner peace.

Few of us can fully appreciate the terrible conspiracy of noise there is about us, noise that denies us the silence and solitude we need for this cultivation of the inner garden. It would not be hard to believe that the archenemy of God has conspired to surround us at every conceivable point in our lives with the interfering noises of civilization that, when left unmuffled, usually drown out the voice of God. One who walks with God will tell you plainly, God does not ordinarily shout to make Himself heard. As Elijah discovered, God tends to whisper in the garden.

I recall a visit to a missionary center in Latin America where workmen were constructing a sound studio for a radio station. They were taking careful measures to soundproof the rooms so that no noise from the city streets could mar the broadcasts and recordings that would emanate from that place. We must learn to soundproof the heart against the intruding noises of the public world in order to hear what God has to say. I love the words of Mother Teresa of Calcutta:

> We need to find God, and he cannot be found in noise and restlessness. *God is the friend of silence.* See how nature—trees, flowers, grass—grow in silence; see the stars, the moon and sun, how they move in silence . . . the more we receive in silent prayer, the more we can give in our active life. *We need silence to be able to touch souls.* The essential thing is not what we say, but what *God* says to us and through us. All our words will be useless unless they come from within—words which do not give the light of Christ increase the darkness.[2]

Our worlds are filled with the noise of endless music, chatter, and busy schedules. In most homes there is a television in almost every room. Nowadays watching a TV program or movie can be done in the car, office, or elevator, on our laps or in our hands. When I dial a friend at his office, I am offered music over the phone until he comes to answer my call. There are cell phones with Beethoven's Ninth Symphony theme as a ringtone, iPods with mega-bass, MP3s and MP4s all invading the mind with noise. Pretty noise, most of the time. But, nevertheless, noise. With the intrusion of so much noise, when can we withdraw and monitor the still, small voice of God?

We are so accustomed to noise that we grow restless without it. Worshipers in a congregation find it difficult to sit in quietness for more than a minute or two; we assume something has gone wrong and someone has forgotten his assignment. Most of us would find it difficult to go even an hour without saying anything or hearing a word from someone.

The struggle can be the same in the experience of solitude. Not only are we often bothered by silence, but few of us are comfortable with times of aloneness. But there must be times of rhythmic withdrawal. There must be those moments when we break from routines, from other relationships, from the demands of the outer world to meet Him in the garden. It cannot be done in large meetings and spectacular celebrations.

Nouwen quotes Thomas Merton, a student of those strange mystics of the early Christian centuries who sometimes pursued solitude to an extreme. What he says about them is instructive. Why did they seek solitude?

> They knew that they were helpless to do any good for others as long as they floundered about in the wreckage [of humanity]. But once they got a foothold on solid ground, things were different. Then they had not only the power but even the obligation to pull the whole world to safety after them.[3]

It is interesting that God's angel used silence to curb the impossible thinking of aged Zacharias, when told that he and his wife were to become the parents of John the Baptizer. If Zacharias could not accept the promise of God as it had come to him, then his tongue would be stilled for several months, and he could think about it. When Elizabeth, his wife, on the other hand, realized what was happening, she withdrew, the Scripture says, partially because that was the custom of pregnant women but also, I believe, because she needed to meditate on the strange and mysterious things that were happening.

Then there was Mary, who, when she learned of her role in the birth of our Lord, did not blurt out all of God's plans, but chose silence. "Mary treasured all these things, pondering them in her heart" (Luke 2:19). Christ's coming was heralded not only by singing and praise from angels but also by silence from human partners who needed solitude in order to think through and appreciate the wonder.

Wayne Oates tells us,

> Silence is not native to my world. Silence, more than likely, is a stranger to your world, too. If you and I ever have silence in our noisy hearts, we are going to have to grow it . . . You can nurture silence in your noisy heart if you value it, cherish it, and are eager to nourish it.[4]

Silence and solitude have not come easily to me at all. I once equated them with laziness, inaction, and a lack of productivity. The minute I was alone, my mind exploded with a list of things I should do: phone calls to make, papers I should be filing, books unread, sermons unprepared, and people I ought to see.

The slightest noise outside my study door was a massive intrusion to concentration. It seemed as if my hearing became supersensitive, and I could overhear conversations at the other end of our house. My curiosity strained to hear what was being said. Because my study was, for years, near our laundry room, it never seemed to fail that the moment I got into spiritual activity the washing machine would decide the load inside was unbalanced, and its foghorn-like buzzer would go off, insisting that I, since everyone else was upstairs, should come and readjust the wash.

But concentrating even when there was silence became desperately difficult. I learned that I had to warm up, to accept the fact that for about fifteen minutes my mind would do everything it could to resist the solitude. So among the things I did was to start by reading or writing on the subject of my spiritual pursuits. Slowly, it seemed, my conscious mind got the message: We (my mind and I) were going to worship and meditate, and the sooner the mind got in touch with the inner garden on the matter, the better it would be.

I expect that I will fight this battle of solitude and silence for as long as I live. I want to say, however, that as time has gone by, and I have begun to reap the benefits of silent time, there has been a growing hunger for more of it. But still there is that first resistance to overcome. When one is an activist by nature, withdrawal can be hard work. But it is a necessary labor.

For me, silence and solitude are best found in the early morning hours. So it goes in that spot on my calendar before anyone can suggest other purposes for the time. For others, it may be late in the evening. But anyone wanting to bring order to the spiritual sector of the private world must find the place and the time that fits his or her personal temperament.

SINGING

I have learned much about God and His touch on my private world through singing. I cannot be thankful enough for the place music has played in my life.

If I begin to dwell on the sadness of my childhood, it is not long before a more positive memory comes to mind. I visualize my mother and father sharing the piano bench in our living room and playing Christian songs. In such moments, all their sorrows and differences seem to dissipate, and they became lost in the music they played together.

I would sit behind them on the couch of our living room listening, wishing there was a way I could join in. Such beautiful music, such a momentary bliss for two people who, at other times, caused each other so much hurt. Music was their binder. And it seemed to me, even as a child, that this was Jesus' gift to them.

When my father and mother were finished, I would climb up

on the piano bench and attempt to replicate what they had just played. As time went by, I learned to play the piano by ear (as they say). I guess it was my personal effort to enter into their occasional experiences of happiness.

Our church was a singing church. We sang the classical Christian hymns and the old gospel songs:

Crown Him with many crowns, the Lamb upon His
    throne . . .[5]
Great is Thy faithfulness! Morning by morning new
    mercies I see . . .[6]
My Jesus, I love thee, I know thou art mine . . .[7]
Rescue the perishing, care for the dying; Jesus is merciful . . .[8]
When we all get to heaven, what a day of rejoicing that
    will be . . .[9]
Then sings my soul, my Savior God, to thee: How great
    thou art . . .[10]

The songs were sung in four parts: soprano, alto, bass, and tenor. When singing, we the congregation became a grand choir, and we imagined Jesus to be the audience. In the making of the music we became unified (from very young to very old) in our faith. We loved the sound we made, and we felt satisfied that Jesus heard us.

Some years ago I was traveling in Southern Russia with a Christian pastor. He knew no English; I knew no Russian. We were left to travel mile after mile in his car in silence.

Then I had a brainstorm of sorts. I began to sing "Blessed Assurance." Almost immediately my traveling friend joined me in his language. We sang all three verses together. And when we finished, he began to sing "O for a Thousand Tongues to Sing." Of course, I joined him.

For the next hour we sang and sang. I have rarely been so thankful for all the songs I learned when I was younger. They became the connection that brought two Christian brothers to the feet of Jesus.

It was the songs of our faith that infused us with a sense of the biblical gospel:

> *Living, He loved me; dying, He saved me;*
> *Buried, He carried my sins far away;*
> *Rising, He justified freely forever:*
> *One day He's coming, O glorious day!*[11]

These songs—hundreds of them—remain deep within me today. When I am alone in the car or walking in the early morning hours, these songs come to the surface one after the other. I sing them. I hear the harmonic parts. I remember the places where I first learned them. And something very "ordering" happens. It's expressed in an old, incredibly simple chorus:

> *Into my heart, into my heart*
> *Come into my heart, Lord Jesus;*
> *Come in today; come in to stay*[12]

A new kind of music is being sung in most churches today, and it's okay even if I miss the songs of my childhood. I applaud the writing and playing efforts of a new generation. But if we are not careful, there could be a problem. Years ago my generation sang our songs thousands of times over. They were drilled into the deepest parts of our private worlds. Most songs today are sung just a few times before they disappear. Sometimes I fear that there may come a day when Christ-following people, like Howard Rutledge, may find themselves in POW camps and have nothing to sing.

LISTENING TO GOD

It must have been like a cold shower on an early morning for Moses as he came off the mountain, after having been with God, and found his Hebrew people dancing around a golden calf. For days he had lived in the presence of holiness itself, and a sense of God's glory and righteousness had been burned into his spirit. But now this spectacle! He was heartbroken.

How had it happened? While Moses had been listening to God, his brother, Aaron, high priest of all the people, had been listening to the people. The input the two received was decidedly different. When Moses listened, he received God's revelation of the law of righteousness. When Aaron listened, he heard complaints, wishes, and demands. Moses brought with him uncompromised standards of heaven; Aaron caved in to the whims of men. *It was all in the listening.*

The garden of our private worlds is cultivated not only when we draw apart for times of silence and solitude but also when we begin, in that environment, to deliberately practice the discipline of listening. I have not met many who know how to listen to God. Busy people find it hard to learn how. Most Christ-followers learned at an early age how to talk to God, but they did not learn to listen as well.

We listen every time we open the Scriptures and place ourselves at the feet of the inspired writers who unfold the mysteries of God. We listen, as I shall point out later on, when we sensitize ourselves to the proddings of God's indwelling Holy Spirit. Listening happens when the preacher or teacher of Scripture, empowered by God's Spirit, brings instruction.

All these things are worth discussing (not to mention doing!). But right now I would like to talk about another exercise, one that can form a base for all the other ways of listening.

It was something I'd longed to do myself, but each time I found it difficult to sustain my effort for more than a few days. But then, on the meltdown day to which I have referred more than a few times in this book, I had this thought: *If I really want to order my private world, I'm going to have to preserve the ways God is speaking to me.*

Toward the end of that day, I acquired a spiral-bound notebook and wrote my first words of reflection.

"Writing organizes and clarifies our thoughts," writes William Zinsser:

> Writing is how we think our way into a subject and make it our own. Writing enables us to find out what we know—and what we don't know—about whatever we're trying to learn. Putting an idea into written words is like defrosting the windshield: The idea, so vague out there in the murk, slowly begins to gather itself into a sensible shape. Whatever we write—a memo, a letter, a note to the baby-sitter—all of us know this moment of finding out what we really want to say by trying in writing to say it.[13]

When I first began to journal, I felt self-conscious. I had visions of everyone stealing a peek at what I was writing . . . and laughing. I had fears that my journal would reveal what I was sure everyone already suspected: that I was a shallow person.

But slowly my reluctances lost their hold on me, and I found myself recording in the journal, more and more, the thoughts that flooded my inner spirit. Into the journal went words describing my feelings, my fears and sense of weakness, my hopes, and my discoveries about where Christ was leading me. When I felt empty or defeated, I wrote about that too.

Slowly I began to realize that journaling was helping me come to grips with an enormous part of my inner person that I had never been fully honest about. No longer could fears and struggles remain inside without definition. They were surfaced and named. And I became aware, little by little, that God's Holy Spirit was directing many of the thoughts and insights as I wrote. On paper, I felt that God and I were carrying on a personal communion. He was helping me, in the words of David, to "search my heart." He was prodding me to put words to my fears, shapes to my doubts. And when I was candid about it, then there would often come out of Scripture or from the meditations of my own heart the reassurances, the rebukes, and the admonishments that I so badly needed. But this began to happen only when the journal was employed.

Because I found that my prayers often seemed disconnected and that I was not able to concentrate (or even stay awake), I often wondered if I could ever develop a vigorous worship and intercessory life. Again, the journal provided a vehicle for writing prayers when my spoken prayers lacked cohesiveness. Now prayer content became sensible, and I began to enjoy recording my progress as a believer and a follower of Christ.

A key contribution of the journal became its record of not only the good moments but the bad times as well. When there came times of discouragement, even of despair, I was able to describe my feelings and tell how God's Spirit ultimately ministered to me to strengthen my resolve. These became special passages to look back on; they helped me celebrate the power of God in the midst of my own weakness.

In days past I wrote of our children as they grew up in our home. The stories of their athletic activities, their first dates, when they got their driver's licenses, the various graduations: they're all there. Our intimate conversations, my dreams and worries about them, my unbounded delight in their growth in character: that's there too. And now the journals say a lot about grandchildren who have come along to bless our lives.

As I said before, I include prayers if I feel like writing them down, insights that come from reading the Bible and other spiritual literature, and concerns I have about my own personal behavior. I love to record things I am seeing in the lives of members of my family. I anticipate that someday our children and grandchildren will read through some of these journals, and if I can posthumously affirm them for things I see in their growing lives today, it will be a treasure for them.

All of this is part of listening to God. As I write, I am aware that what I am writing may actually be what God wants to tell me. I dare to presume that His Spirit is often operative in the things I am choosing to think about and record. And it becomes important to search my heart to see what conclusions He may be engendering, what matters He wishes to remind me about, what themes He hopes to stamp upon my private world.

I am reminded that the Lord once had the Israelites save "two quarts of manna" (Ex. 16:33 TLB) so that they would have a tangible reminder of His constant care. The journal became my "two quarts," for in it I had all the testimony I needed to the faithfulness of God in my life. This remembering process, which a journal provides, is very significant.

In these last forty-eight years, I have acquired a positive addiction to journaling. Hardly a morning passes that I do not open the journal and record the things I hear God saying through my reading, meditation, and daily experience. When the journal is opened, the ear of my heart is opened too. If God is going to speak, I am ready to listen.

How to Journal

When I have spoken in public on journaling, I have found that people are intensely interested and have many questions. Their initial curiosity tends to center on technique more than anything else. What does your journal look like? How often do you write in it?

What sorts of things do you include? Isn't it really just a diary? Do you let your wife read your journal? Although I am by no means an expert journal keeper, I endeavor to answer as best I can.

For many years my journals were simple spiral-bound notebooks that I purchased at an office-supply store. They were rather unimpressive in appearance. I filled one of them with about three months of horrendous handwriting. Many years later, when I acquired my first personal computer, I began to type my journal. Every few weeks I printed out the file and had two hundred or so pages bound. Today, I imagine there are more than a hundred of these volumes.

I write in my journal almost every day, but I am not overly concerned if an occasional day passes without an entry. I have made it a habit to write in the earliest moments of my time of spiritual exercise, and, for me, that means the first thing in the morning. A typical entry includes an account of things that I accomplished in the preceding day, people I met, things I learned, feelings I experienced, and impressions I believe God wanted me to have.

Occasionally someone asks, "What would an entry in your journal sound like?" I'm not overly comfortable opening up my journal for others to examine. Many of its pages are rather private, you understand. But I did look through a journal from years ago and came up with this sample for those who are constructively curious.

I find myself dreading the 6 A.M. news each morning because the world is in such terrible shape right now. I think back two years ago when we dared to dream that the Israeli/ Palestinian conflict just might be headed toward resolution. But today! I can hardly remember any moment when things have been worse, when the two sides hated each other more. What a terrible, terrible waste of human life. An entire generation of children and young people being raised to hate. Please, Father: divine intervention!

My Bible reading this morning is from Matthew 6. The first half of the chapter focuses on giving and praying. All to be done, basically, in secret. Nothing designed to impress anybody. Clearly, Jesus is disturbed by the tendency then (and now?) to make a big deal out of these religious disciplines so that the effort becomes something intended to impress people more than to align one's heart with God.

"Be careful not to do your 'acts of righteousness' before men, to be seen by them." I've been thinking while reading this about our habit of self-analysis, something a tad different from self-examination. Not only are we tempted to "perform" for others, but we sometimes perform for ourselves. Even as I pray, for example, I sometimes find myself analyzing the quality of my own prayer. Does it sound "saintly" enough? Could I have said it better?

Even as I give or serve, I sometimes find myself watching and critiquing myself, wondering how it comes across to others. Such is the complexity of spiritual life, the garbledness of so much we do. I'm challenged once again to assure that my motives and purposes are examined for unsoundness.

I must be sure that Gail knows how much I appreciate her attentiveness to me over the last few days. We have had some wonderful laughs together. Yesterday we spent a couple of hours cleaning up winter debris in the front field. She raked, and I put the leaves and sticks through the chipper. Now Gail has plenty of stuff for her mulching operation. She was delighted. Not hard to make her happy. This year I'm committed to liking yard work more.

My journal also becomes a repository of quotes and insights that come from my Bible reading and the books I am going through at the time. If a comment by an author stands out, I like to copy it into the journal (in boldface) so the very exercise of typing it out stamps it more deeply into my mind. It is a fascinating experience to page back through a journal, from a year or two ago, and see all the thoughts that were influencing me in those moments.

Thumbing through a recent journal, I discovered a page that contains quotations from one of Henri Nouwen's oldest books: "Reading from Nouwen this morning. He writes about conversations with the juggler and tight rope walker, Philippe Petit. When he was asked why he did these things, he answered, 'If I see three oranges, I have to juggle. And if I see two towers, I have to walk.'" At the end of this quote I wrote: "Gmac [my initials]. This is good for a talk on the subject of call or mission."

My journals are not heavy with merely serious spiritual reflections or intellectual musings. They are also a place where I enjoy recording the light things of life. Again, something out of a journal that is many, many years old.

> The baseball season has started today, and the Red Sox have lost their first game to Toronto. Pedro Martinez was humiliated for 7 or 8 runs and an unthinkable number of hits. The NCAA championship game was played last evening, and Gail and I sat up and watched it. Maryland over Indiana! And, believe it or not, the Patriots have begun early season workouts. Do I have to start worrying about defending the Super Bowl championship this soon? So the world plays while the Middle East heats up and unravels.

Journal-keeping becomes a habit for most people if they will stick with it for the better part of a year. Most people quit too quickly, never achieving the habit pattern, and that is unfortunate.

I am careful to keep a journal even when I am traveling. It helps me to maintain a record of those I have met, so that when I return again to places where I have visited, I can simply review my previous visit in the journal and pick up relationships where they may have been suspended due to distance.

Since I first wrote about journaling, it has fascinated me to see how many people have written books about the subject. One could probably go to any religious bookstore and find several dozen books about keeping a journal. When I have leafed through some of them, I've been disappointed with those who tried to reduce this effort—as in a lot of spiritual disciplines—to systems and gimmickry. But the proliferation of literature on journaling suggests that more and more people are seeking a way to gain perspective and meaning on lives caught up in a torrent of demands, noises, and distractions. If a journal can help to give shape to a quiet period in one's daily life, then let it be so.

Looking back on my almost fifty years of journaling, I can tell you that establishing the discipline was among the most important decisions of my life. I have a record of the faithfulness of God, the greatest and the darkest moments of my life, the story of my family and my friends, the tidbits from innumerable books. The dozens of journals that sit in that safe are wealth to me.

My mind goes back to Howard Rutledge in his prison camp. Every voice was a hostile one; every noise introduced the possibility of something about to go wrong. In such an ugly place, was there a friendly voice, a lovely sound to be heard anywhere? Yes, if you had trained your ears to hear in the inner garden. There the greatest of all sounds may be heard: those belonging to Him who seeks our companionship and growth. In the words of an old and very sentimental hymn,

> He speaks, and the sound of His voice
> Is so sweet the birds hush their singing.
> —C. AUSTIN MILES, "IN THE GARDEN"[14]

TWELVE

EVERYTHING HAS
TO BE ENTERED

ON HIS DEATHBED, IN GREAT DISCOMFORT AND BARELY ABLE TO COM-
municate, E. Stanley Jones managed to dictate some final thoughts
that summed up his Christian journey. Employing the metaphor of
a mountain climber's rope to describe the toughness of his spirit,
he said, "The innermost strands are the strongest." Noble words,
these. Worth one's pause and reflection.

Despite such courage, Jones would have been the first to
acknowledge that it had not always been that way. In the early days
of his life and ministry there had come a temporary sinkhole collapse. For more than a year he had languished in both spiritual and
physical ineffectiveness. "The spiritual sag brought on a physical
sag," he remembered. "The outer collapse took place because the
inner experience could not sustain it. I had made it a life motto that
I would not preach what I was not experiencing, so the outer and
the inner came together in collapse."[1]

When an old saint—now with the Lord—makes it a point to
recall difficult days on the spiritual journey, it's time to listen. He
offers a caution to younger men and women. He is telling us that
no matter how good life might be at any one moment, tests of the

"inner strands" are only a matter of time. Jones and people like him who finished their lives with great spiritual strength did not get that way by simply staying busy. They understood the priority of spiritual discipline.

The discipline of the spirit—what I have called the cultivation of the inner garden—depends on the willingness of men and women of Christ to seek solitude and silence and to listen for the whisper of God.

But the things that we hear in solitude and silence must be internalized. Years ago, when I wrote the first edition of *Ordering Your Private World,* a lot of us were just beginning to become familiar with the personal computer. When I bravely purchased one of the first IBM PCs, I thought it would revolutionize my way of writing and of storing and retrieving information I needed for sermons and books. But figuring out how to use the computer was a huge task. No one really knew how the things worked. Even that salesman who sold me the bulky machine and printer (for $7,200) could barely describe how to switch it on, let alone boot up the word processing program. I would have to find out for myself.

It took me almost three weeks to figure out how to use the computer even in the most basic sense. One of the first things I had to get used to was the function of the Enter key. The teaching manual instructed me that I could type anything I wanted on the screen in front of me. But until I hit the Enter key, the computer would not "hear" or respond to a single word I had typed. All of my words, no matter how impressive, would just sit on the screen's surface until I entered them onto a file in the heart (the "memory") of the computer.

It occurred to me that this was not unlike my listening processes, for I have the ability to hear things, *but that does not necessarily mean that everything enters or penetrates my heart.*

Salvation Army commissioner Samuel Logan Brengle, speaking of his spiritual disciplines, wrote,

I do a lot of listening. Prayer, you know, is not meant to be a monologue, but a dialogue. It is a communion, a friendly talk. While the Lord communicates with me mainly through His Word, He gives me a great deal of comfort in a direct manner. By "comfort" I do not mean cuddling or coddling but *assurance*—assurance of His presence with me and His pleasure in my service. It is like the comfort given by a military commander to his soldier or envoy whom he sends on a difficult mission: "You go, put on your armor, I'm watching you, and I'll send you all the reinforcements you need as they are needed." I have to be comforted that way a great deal. I don't just assume that God is near me and pleased with me; I must have a fresh witness daily.[2]

The Bible tells of another Samuel, a young boy interning in the tabernacle under the discipleship of Eli, the high priest. During the night, Samuel heard a voice calling his name. Running to Eli's bed, he assumed that he was being summoned for some task. But Eli had not called, and Samuel returned to his room. But the call came again and again. It was Eli who put things together and suggested how Samuel could respond the next time. "Go lie down, and it shall be if He [the voice] calls you, that you shall say, 'Speak, LORD, for Your servant is listening'" (1 Sam. 3:9). In others words, Samuel, push the Enter key.

Samuel did, and God spoke. The words of God penetrated his heart and changed his destiny. We strengthen the innermost strands, as Jones put it, by making sure that God's words are entering the garden of our private worlds. Our first step in spiritual discipline is finding solitude and silence; the second step is learning to listen to God. The third step, the pushing of the Enter key, is done through *reflection and meditation*.

Some Christians are uneasy and negative about the mention of such words. They think such practices can open a door to activity that is too undirected and that can lead to misguided conclusions. They conjure up images of people sitting in lotus positions and engaging in trancelike activities.

But the Bible is full of reflective or meditative passages and calls us to open our private worlds to them. Among the most popular are those passages out of the Psalms, where the writer fixes his mind on certain aspects of God's being and consistent care for His children.

The psalmist looked through all sorts of meditative lenses. For example, he saw God as a shepherd, as a commanding general, and as a director of spiritual exercise.

The act of meditation is like tuning the spirit to heavenly frequencies. We take a portion of Scripture and simply allow it to enter into the deepest recesses of self. There are often several different results: cleansing, reassurance, and the desire to praise and give thanksgiving. Sometimes meditation on something of God's nature or His actions opens our minds to new guidance or a new awareness of something the Lord may be trying to say to us.

In his book of prayers, John Baillie reveals a meditational mood when he prays:

> Almighty God, in this quiet hour I seek communion with thee. From the fret and fever of the day's business, from the world's discordant noises, from the praise and blame of men, from the confused thoughts and vain imaginations of my own heart, I would now turn aside and seek the quietness of thy presence. All day long have I toiled and striven; but now in the stillness of heart and the clear light of thine eternity, I would ponder the pattern my life is weaving.[3]

Meditation, of course, can be done only when we have chosen an environment where there will be adequate amounts of time, silence, and privacy. One does not get much meditation done on a bus or when driving in traffic—although I have heard people claim that was their time for the spiritual discipline.

Many of us will discover that it takes preparatory time in order to meditate. You may have had the experience of coming in from heavy exercise still breathing very hard. You know that it is virtually impossible to sit down for several minutes and be still. There is too much gasping and catching of breath for quiet sitting. The same is true in reflection. We often enter the chamber to meet with God while we are still emotionally out of breath. It is hard at first to concentrate our thoughts and to bring them into the presence of the Lord. We have to quietly relax for a short season while the mind accustoms itself to spiritual activity in the "garden" environment. Thus, it will take time—time some people are reluctant to give.

Christ-followers have always considered the Bible to be the central revelation of our faith and worthy of meditation. Let me add that reading the great classics of Christian literature is a must for spiritual growth. Down through the centuries there have been men and women who have recorded their insights and exercises for us to read. And although these books do not carry the authoritative power of the Bible, they nevertheless contain an enormous amount of spiritual food.

Reflection and meditation demand a certain amount of imagination. We read the first psalm, for example, and picture a tree planted by a river. What is true about that tremendous tree to which the writer likens the man or woman who walks after God? In Psalm 19 we let our minds sweep across the universe and imagine the celestial bodies and their incredible message. When we read the passages describing Jesus' ministry, our reflecting minds place ourselves right into the story. We see the Savior heal, hear Him teach, and respond to His directives. In meditation we latch on to phrases from the prophets, perhaps memorizing small portions, and we allow the words to trickle down over the structures of our inner being as we repeat them over and over again. From such exercises come new and wonderful conclusions. The word of God is *entering* our private worlds. And because we have fixed our attention on His word, we can be sure the Holy Spirit will guide our meditations.

C. S. Lewis, writing to an American friend, spoke of reflective exercises:

We all go through periods of dryness in our prayers, don't we? I doubt whether they are necessarily a bad symptom. I sometimes suspect that what we *feel* to be our best prayers are really our worst; that what we are enjoying is the satisfaction of apparent success, as in executing a dance or reciting a poem. Do our prayers sometimes go wrong because we insist on trying to talk to God when He wants to talk with us? Joy tells me that once, years ago, she was haunted one morning by a feeling that God wanted something of her, a persistent pressure like the nag of a neglected duty. And till mid-morning she kept on wondering what it was. But the moment she stopped worrying, the answer came through as plain as a spoken voice. It was "I don't want you to *do* anything. I want to *give* you something"; and immediately her heart was peace and delight. St. Augustine says, "God gives where He finds empty hands." A man whose hands are full of parcels can't receive a gift. Perhaps these parcels are not always sins or earthly cares, but sometimes our own fussy attempts to worship Him in *our* way. Incidentally, what most often interrupts my own prayers is not great distractions but tiny ones—things one will have to do or avoid in the course of the next hour.[4]

Here is a good example of the exercise of reflection and meditation. God speaks, we listen, and the message is entered within the heart. The need for outer props is lessened; the inner garden is further cultivated. The man or woman of spiritual discipline is growing strong in the private world.

THIRTEEN

SEEING THROUGH HEAVEN'S EYES

IN AN INSIGHTFUL LITTLE BOOK ON CONTEMPLATIVE FAITH WRITTEN more than ninety years ago, a European Christian by the name of Bridget Herman wrote:

> When we read the lives of the saints, we are struck by a certain large leisure which went hand in hand with a remarkable effectiveness. They were never hurried; they did comparatively few things, and these not necessarily striking or important; and they troubled very little about their influence. Yet they always seemed to hit the mark; every bit of their life told; their simplest actions had a distinction, an exquisiteness which suggested the artist. The reason is not far to seek. Their sainthood lay in their habit of referring the smallest actions to God. They lived in God; they acted from a pure motive of love towards God. They were as free from self-regard as from slavery to the good opinion of others. God saw and God rewarded: what else needed they? They possessed God and possessed themselves in God. Hence the inalienable dignity of these meek, quiet figures

that seem to produce such marvelous effects with such humble materials.[1]

The fifth way we can enhance communion with God in the garden of our private worlds is through *prayer as worship and intercession*. This is what Bridget Herman said characterized the saints: "Their sainthood lay in their habit of referring the smallest actions to God."

"Let inward prayer be your last act before you fall asleep and the first act when you awake," Thomas Kelly wrote. "And in time you will find, as did Brother Lawrence, that 'those who have the gale of the Holy Spirit go forward even in sleep.'"[2]

Most of us have never experienced this. Daily, disciplined prayer is one of the most difficult exercises Christ-followers undertake.

Married men will often admit, for example, that praying with their wives is a very difficult thing. Why? They really don't have an answer. Sometimes pastors in a moment of self-revelation will reveal that the integrity of their prayer lives is usually an embarrassment to them. And they also are hard pressed to explain it.

My impression after visiting with many Christ-followers is that worship and intercession rank at the top of any list of spiritual struggles. No one would deny that prayer is important, but few believe their prayer lives to be adequately developing. And this is a major reason the inner gardens of so many private worlds are in a state of disorder. It is why most of us would have a hard time saying, like E. Stanley Jones, "No outer props are necessary."

WHY WE HAVE TROUBLE PRAYING

Why do so many people have struggles when it comes to prayer? Let me suggest three possible reasons.

Worship and Intercession Seem to Be Unnatural Acts

Men and women were originally created to desire communion with God. But the effects of sin have dulled most of that original human desire. Sin turned a natural activity into an unnatural function.

My suspicion is that when sin affected man so deeply, it touched his spiritual dimensions most severely of all, while leaving the original physical appetites and desires virtually undiminished. Our instinctive preoccupations with food, sexual pleasure, and security are probably close to their original levels. It may be helpful to speculate that man in his sinless nature once probably had as great, if not greater, desire for communion with the Creator as he has for the satisfaction of the natural and very real appetites and instincts that we live with today. But the spiritual hunger, once undoubtedly powerful, has been terribly dulled by the power of sin. Thus, worship and intercession have become difficult challenges.

As a result, praying in any meaningful way goes against virtually everything within our natural selves and is foreign to what our culture teaches us as a way of life.

And that is the heart of the trouble. Few people realize how brainwashed each of us is. Messages bombard our private worlds every day, telling us that anything of a spiritual nature is a waste of time. From our earliest years we are subtly taught that the only way to achieve anything is through action. But prayer seems to be a form of inaction. To the person with a disordered private world, it does not seem to accomplish anything.

Until we believe that prayer is indeed a real and highly significant activity, that it does, in fact, reach beyond space and time to the God who is actually there, we will never acquire the habits of worship and intercession. To gain these habits, we must make a conscious effort to overcome the part of us that thinks that praying is not a natural part of life.

Worship and Intercession Are Tacit
Admissions of Weakness

A second reason people find it difficult to enter into worship and intercession is that these acts are by nature admissions of personal weakness. In the act of prayer, something within the inner garden acknowledges that we are utterly dependent on the One to whom we address our words.

Now, we can *say* that we are weak people, and we can *say* that we depend on God for all of our sustenance; but the fact is something in us is not willing to *recognize* it. There is something deep within that vigorously denies our dependence.

As I mentioned earlier, I have often been fascinated with the reluctance of many Christian men to pray with their wives or feel free to take prayer leadership in a mixed group. It is not unusual for a Christian wife to complain, "My husband never prays with me, and I can't understand it."

The answer may lie in the fact that men have been taught in our culture never to reveal weakness or engage in any activity that may show it. Prayer in its most authentic form acknowledges that we are weak and dependent on our God. Something in the male knows this and unconsciously fights having to identify with the fact of dependence.

It is my observation that most women, on the other hand, at least until recently, have never had to struggle to face their own weaknesses; and that may be one reason that, as a group, they feel more at ease in prayer than men. Generalizations, these, of course. But may I be frank? The generalizations about men and women at prayer are pretty consistent.

A person shows significant spiritual growth when he finds it possible to admit that he needs a relationship with God in order to be the human being he was created to be. There is an enormous sense of liberation in that realization.

Brother Lawrence wrote,

> We must examine with care what are the virtues of which we stand most in need, what are those which are most difficult to win, the sins to which we most often fall, and the most frequent and inevitable occasions of our falling. We must turn to God in complete confidence in the hour of battle, abide strongly in the presence of his divine majesty, worship him humbly, and set before him our woes and our weaknesses. And thus we shall find in him all virtues though we may lack them all.[3]

Brother Lawrence seemed never to have any problems facing up to his weaknesses, and that is one reason his prayer life was so alive.

Prayer Sometimes Seems to Be Unrelated to Actual Results

A third reason prayer comes hard to us is the fact that it seems frequently unrelated to actual results. Lest you think I am guilty of denying a substantial teaching of Scripture, hear me carefully. I do, in fact, believe that God answers prayer. But most of us have had enough experience to realize that His answers do not always come in forms or on schedules that we would have designed.

As a very young pastor, I recall acknowledging my confusion about this matter of personal prayer to my wife. "Sometimes it seems as if, on those weeks when I pray very little, my sermons come out very powerful. And on those weeks when I feel that I've really done my prayer work, I seem to preach my worst. Now you tell me," I'd challenge her, "what does God expect me to do when He doesn't seem to give me, pound for pound, the blessings that match my prayer investment?"

Like others, I have prayed for healings, for miracles, for guidance, and for assistance. Frankly, there were times I was sure God would answer me because I had mustered strong feelings of faith. But many of those times nothing happened—or if it did, it was entirely unlike what I had anticipated.

We live in a society that is reasonably organized. Put a letter in the box, and it usually ends up where you want it to go. Order an item on the Internet, and it usually comes to you in the right size, color, and model. Ask someone to provide you a service, and it is reasonable to expect that it will work out that way. In other words, we are used to results in response to our arrangements. That is why prayer can be discouraging for some of us. How can we predict the result? We are tempted to abandon prayer as a viable exercise and to try getting the results ourselves.

But the fact is that my prayer life cannot be directly tied to the results I expect or demand. I have had many opportunities by now to see that the things I want God to do in response to my prayers can be unhealthy for me. I have begun to see that worship and intercession are far more the business of aligning myself with God's purposes than asking Him to align with mine.

Henri Nouwen said it best when he once wrote,

> Prayer is a radical conversion of all our mental processes because in prayer we move away from ourselves, our worries, preoccupation, and self-gratification—and direct all that we recognize as ours to God in the simple trust that through his love all will be made new.[4]

When our Lord came to the garden on the night of His crucifixion, His prayer just before His capture centered on affirming His oneness with the Father's purposes. This is mature praying.

Many times I have gone to prayer with results in mind. I wanted to gain control over the people and events I was praying about by dictating to the Father my views on how things should come out.

When I do this, I am looking at people and events through an earthly lens, not a heavenly one. I am praying as though I know better than God what the best outcome is.

Thomas Kelly suggests that a more proper kind of prayer is, "Lord, be Thou my will." Perhaps among the purest prayers we can pray is simply to ask, "Father, may I see earth through heaven's eyes."

Again Kelly wrote,

> The life that intends to be wholly obedient, wholly submissive, wholly listening, is astonishing in its completeness. Its joys are ravishing, its peace profound, its humility the deepest, its power world shaking, its love enveloping, its simplicity that of a trusting child.[5]

It was this kind of thinking that helped me overcome the obstacles to worship and intercession that have often been quite real to me. Yes, praying is unnatural for the natural man. But Christ has entered life, and what once was unnatural now becomes natural, if I ask for the power to make it so. Yes, praying signals weakness and dependence. But that is the truth about me, and I am healthier for coming to grips with it. And yes, the answers to my prayers do not always coincide with my expectations. But the problem is in my expectations—not in the capacities or sensitivities of God.

Having encountered these obstacles, how do we develop the discipline of worship and intercession in the garden?

VISITING WITH GOD

The practical side of worship and intercession has to do with *time*—when to pray; *posture*—how to pray; and *content*—what to include during visits with the Father.

All of us will find different parts of the day best for our spiritual disciplines. I am a morning person; but one of my closest friends tells me that he finds the evening hours best. Whereas I begin the day in prayer, he ends it that way. Neither of us has airtight arguments for his choice; I think it is a matter of individual rhythms. Daniel of Babylon solved the problem by being a morning and an evening person—and a noontime person too.

When I come to the morning hour, I find it virtually impossible to enter into worship or intercession the moment I come to my private place of solitude. Remember the out-of-breath principle? Praying with a fully active mind fresh from a host of conversations and decisions is difficult, if not impossible. To pray meaningfully, the mind has to be slowed down to a reflective pace.

In order to make this happen, I often begin by reading or writing in my journal. This sort of thing will slowly convince my mind that I am really serious about spiritual exercise, and so it is less liable to rebel when I turn toward prayer.

Is there a prime posture for prayer? Probably not, although some would like to make us think so. In the biblical cultures, people were most likely to stand while they prayed. However, the very word *prayer* from the Old Testament means to prostrate oneself, and that may mean at times full length upon the floor.

Friends of A. W. Tozer, a great man of prayer in our time, tell me that he had a pair of coveralls in the closet in his study. When he came to the moments of prayer in his day, he put them on and stretched out upon the hard floor. The coveralls, of course, prevented him from getting his dress clothes dirty. Although one or two may find it out of place to say this, the fact is that the Muslim posture for prayer is worth trying. This is done by kneeling and then leaning forward until one's forehead is touching the floor. I have found that when I am tired, the Muslim posture helps me to be mentally and spiritually alert.

Sometimes I pray while pacing back and forth in my study; on other occasions I am content simply to sit. The point is that prayer can be carried on in all different postures—and perhaps it is best to assume all of them from one time to another.

Serious intercessors keep prayer lists. Although I am not implying that I call myself a serious intercessor, I do keep one, usually on index cards that I can keep close to me. They help me to review my chief concerns as I pray. It's the only way I know of making sure that those for whom God has given me a burden are responsibly lifted up as an expression of my love and caring.

THE CONTENT OF PRAYER

What should we pray about? Take a look at an excerpt from the prayers of Samuel Logan Brengle, an evangelist of the Salvation Army at the beginning of the twentieth century:

> Keep me, O Lord, from waxing mentally and spiritually dull and stupid. Help me to keep the physical, mental, and spiritual fiber of the athlete, of the man who denies himself daily and takes up his cross and follows Thee. Give me good success in my work, but hide pride from me. Save me from the self-complacency that so frequently accompanies success and prosperity. Save me from the spirit of sloth, of self-indulgence, as physical infirmities and decay creep upon me.[6]

No wonder Brengle was effective. He knew how and what to pray for. There was nothing held back, even in a short piece of intercession like this one. Having recorded this prayer, Brengle's biographer adds: "Thus praying daily and hourly, the prophet kept his passion hot and his eye single, even as he came down the decline."[7]

Adoration

In our spiritual disciplines when we visit with the Father in the inner garden, adoration ought to be the first item on the worship agenda.

How can we worship in prayer? By first reflecting on who God is and thanking Him for the things He has revealed about Himself. To worship in prayer is to allow our spirits to feast on what God has revealed concerning His acts in the distant and recent past, and what He has told us about Himself. Slowly, as we review these things in a spirit of thanksgiving and recognition, we can sense our spirits beginning to expand, to take in the broader reality of God's presence and being. Slowly our consciousness is able to accept the fact that the universe about us is not closed or limited but is, in fact, as expansive as the Creator meant for it to be. As we enter into worship, we remind ourselves of how great He is.

Confession

In the light of God's majesty, we are called to an honesty about ourselves, what we are by contrast. This is the second aspect of prayer: confession. Spiritual discipline calls for a regular acknowledgement of our true nature and the specific acts and attitudes of the recent past that have not been pleasurable to God as He has sought our fellowship and our obedience.

"God be merciful to me a sinner" is an abbreviated version of the prayer of confession. We need the daily humbling experience of being broken before God as we face up to our imperfection, our propensity to seek evil ways. What has startled me as a Christ-follower has been the constant awareness of new levels of sin that I had not spotted within myself before.

Many years ago, when Gail and I bought the old, abandoned New Hampshire farm we now call Peace Ledge, we found the site where we wished to build our country home strewn with rocks and boulders. It was going to take a lot of hard work to clear it all out so there could be grass and plants. The whole family went to work on the clearing process. The first phase of the clearing project was easy. The big boulders went fast. And when they were gone, we began to see that there were a lot of smaller rocks that had to go too. And so we cleared the area again. But when we had cleared the site of the boulders and rocks, we noticed all of the stones and pebbles we had not seen before. This was much harder, more tedious work. But we stuck to it, and there came a day when the soil was ready for planting grass.

Our private lives are much like that field was. When I first began to follow Christ seriously, He pointed out many major behavior and attitude patterns that, like boulders, had to be removed. And as the years went by, many of those great big boulders did indeed get removed. But when they began to disappear, I discovered a whole new layer of action and attitude in my life that I had not previously seen. But Christ saw them and rebuked them one by one. The removal process began again. Then I reached that point in my Christian life at which Christ and I were dealing with stones and pebbles. They are too numerous to imagine, and as far as I can see, for the rest of my days on earth I will be working with the many stones and pebbles in my life. Every day at spiritual discipline time, there is likely to be a new stab at the clearing process.

But I must not leave this story without noting something else. Every spring at Peace Ledge, after the frost is out of the ground, we found that new stones and boulders appeared around our country home. They had been beneath the surface of the ground, working their way up. And at their appointed times, one by one, they showed up. Some of them were very frustrating to deal with because they looked small until we tried to remove them. And only then did we discover that there was more to those boulders than met the eye.

My sinfulness is exactly the same. It consists of stones, pebbles, and boulders that come to the surface one by one. And the man or woman who ignores the daily experience of confession in spiritual discipline will soon be overwhelmed by them. I understand why the apostle Paul at an advanced age would call himself the "chief of sinners." Even while in jail facing the end of his life, he was still removing pebbles and boulders.

I smile at young believers who tell me that they are discouraged because of all the sin they see in their lives. The fact that they can at least see and feel repelled by that sin shows they are actually growing. There are too many people claiming to be followers of Christ who lost sight of their own sinfulness years ago. If they attend worship on Sunday, they leave without ever having had the experience of brokenness and repentance before God that indicates true worship. This leads to substandard Christianity.

E. Stanley Jones wrote of the importance of confession in our spiritual disciplines:

> I know that there are certain mental and emotional and moral and spiritual attitudes that are anti-health: anger, resentments, fear, worry, desire to dominate, self-preoccupation, guilts, sexual impurity, jealousy, a lack of creative activity, inferiorities, a lack of love. These are the twelve apostles of ill health. *So in prayer I've learned to surrender these things to Jesus Christ as they appear.* I once asked Dr. Kagawa: "What is prayer?" And he answered: "Prayer is self-surrender." I agree. It is primarily self-surrender, blanket surrender, day by day. It is all we know and all we don't know. "All we don't know" covers the unfolding future and involves problems as they arise. So in prayer if any of these twelve things arise, and they do arise, for no one is free from the suggestion of anyone of them, I've learned how to deal with them: not to fight them, but to surrender them to Jesus Christ, and say, "Now, Lord, you have this."[8]

THE MINISTRY OF INTERCESSION

The great prayer warriors all seem to agree that intercession can begin only after we have fully worshiped. Having put ourselves in touch with the living God, we are prepared to pray with what Thomas Kelly called "the eyes of Heaven."

Old Commissioner Brengle was a man of prayer. His biographer wrote,

> At prayer, he was a study in communion. It was his habit, except for those periods when he was too ill, to get out of bed between four and five o'clock in the morning and devote at least a full hour before breakfast to communion with his Lord. Dr. Hayes, whose book, "The Heights of Christian Devotion" carries these dedicatory words: "To Commissioner Samuel Logan Brengle, A Man of Prayer," gives us this glimpse:
>
> "When Brengle has been a guest in my home, I often have found him on his knees with his open Bible on the bed or chair before him, reading his Bible through in that way and saying that the attitude helped him to turn all he read into personal petition: 'O Lord, help me to do this, or not to do that. Help me to be like this man, or to avoid this error.'"[9]

When worship has been completed, intercession can begin. Intercession usually means prayer on behalf of others. It is the greatest single ministry, in my opinion, that the Christian is privileged to have. And perhaps the most difficult.

Have you ever noticed that most faithful intercessors seem to be older people? Why? One reason may be that they have had to simplify their activities. But also note that older people may have become aware that intercession is much more effective than hours of unprayerful activity. And of course, experience through trial and error has taught them the wisdom of leaning on the reliable strength of God.

I have set out in the last few years to master the ministry of intercession for the sake of ministry to others. The progress is slow. Perhaps it is the greatest challenge of my private world.

The greater the spiritual authority and responsibility a person has, the more important it is that he develop intercessory capacities. That takes time and the sort of discipline many of us find difficult.

I think this is what the apostles, the leaders of the early congregation at Jerusalem, were getting at in Acts 6, when they asked for associates to take on the tasks of ministering to the widows and orphans so they could "devote [themselves] to prayer and to the ministry of the word" (v. 4). Note what comes first on the priority list of these busy, busy men. They were starting to miss prayer and were quite nervous about the situation.

Intercession literally means "to stand between two parties and plead the case of one to the other." Is there a greater example of intercession than the prayerful work of Moses, who gave himself to frequent strenuous petition on behalf of the wayward people of Israel?

For whom do we normally intercede? If married, for our spouses and children, obviously. But intercession also means widening the circle to take in close friends, those for whom God has made us responsible, the men and women with whom we work, and those in our congregations and neighborhoods whose personal needs are known to us.

My intercessory list includes many Christian leaders and organizations. There are many whom I know and like, but I must confess that I do not have much more than an occasional prayer burden for them. By contrast, there are some whose needs and pressures are very real to me, and I hold them before the Lord in my intercessory exercise every day. They find it of immense encouragement to hear me say, "I pray for you every day." Being responsible for a certain amount of Christian leadership myself, I have learned how supportive it feels to know that there is a handful of people who hold me before the throne of God in intercession every day.

Intercession means that we must take into account the mandate for world evangelization. In order to systematically pray around the world, I have divided up the continents in such a way that I can pray each day for one of them: Sunday, Latin America; Monday, Central America; Tuesday, North America; Wednesday, Europe; Thursday, Africa; Friday, Asia; and Saturday, the nations of the Pacific. In each area I include intercessions for the national church, for missionaries with whom I am acquainted, and for the terrible suffering people are facing.

We are encouraged to bring our own petitions or requests before the Lord. Somehow I feel that these ought to come last in our prayer activity, but that is purely an opinion. I am thinking of matters in and about my personal life where it seems best to ask God for wisdom and supply. I have struggled with how much I should ask God for (some say everything) and how much He assumes we will handle ourselves. I don't know that I have a good answer to this. I discover as I grow in my faith that I am constrained to ask less and less for myself and more and more for others. And my personal requests tend to be more and more for resources and abilities that would be more of benefit for others.

The gardens within our private worlds cannot remain uncultivated for long before they become infested with the sort of growth that makes them uninviting, both to the indwelling Lord and to us. When neglected for long, they become more like dumps than gardens. And then we have to rely upon external sources of strength and direction to keep moving ahead.

That was the reason for Howard Rutledge's struggle in the North Vietnam prison camp. By God's grace, he testifies, he made it through. But he never forgot what it is like to face such an ordeal when one's private world of the spirit has been left generally uncultivated.

A well-known Christian personality of the past century, Eric Liddell, the Olympic champion runner who was the hero of the movie *Chariots of Fire*, had a remarkably different experience in a prison in North China during World War II. His biographer speaks of the high esteem with which Liddell was held in the Weinsen Camp. And what was the secret of his extraordinary leadership power, his joy, and his integrity in the midst of enormous hardship? The biographer quotes a woman who was in the camp at the time and, with her husband, knew Liddell well:

> What was his secret? Once I asked him, but I really knew already, for my husband was in his dormitory and shared the secret with him. Every morning about 6 a. m., with curtains tightly drawn to keep in the shining of our peanut-oil lamp, lest the prowling sentries would think someone was trying to escape, he used to climb out of his top bunk, past the sleeping forms of his dormitory mates. Then, at the small Chinese table, the two men would sit close together with the light just enough to illumine their Bibles and notebooks. Silently they read, prayed, thought about what should be done. *Eric was a man of prayer not only at set times*—though he did not like to miss a prayer meeting or communion service when such could be arranged. *He talked to God all the time, naturally, as one can who enters the "School of Prayer" to learn this way of inner discipline.* He seemed to have no weighty mental problems: his life was grounded in God, in faith, and in trust.[10]

To bring order to our private worlds is to cultivate the garden as Liddell did. From such exercises, according to the writer of Proverbs (4:23), comes a heart out of which flows life-giving energy.

FOURTEEN

FRIENDS

A DAY OR TWO AGO MY CELL PHONE RANG, AND WHEN I SWIPED THE
screen, I heard the voice of a man I call a Capital-*F* Friend. I have
known this man for almost forty years.

This man is one of only a half-dozen people I refer to as
Capital-*F* Friends. There are many others whose friendship I
greatly value. We have dinners together, share similar interests,
take an interest in each other's children. But Capital-*F* Friends are
different. *They know your heart, and you know theirs.* That takes
time, initiative, and deep caring.

The man on the phone had called to remind me that three of
us Capital-*F* guys were scheduled to get together later in the week
for an entire day. It was going to be a talk day.

And what might we talk about? We'd probably start by talking
about the Red Sox, books we're reading, places we've been. And
we'd probably catch one another up on the news of our children
and grandchildren and other friends we have in common.

But the real topic that would consume most of the day would
be *aging*. We're old guys. We have a lot of things happening in our
lives that no one has prepared us for. So we need to talk about how

we're getting along. Sometimes our bodies rebel against our ambitions. In other words, we want to do more things than we have the durability for.

This is the agenda for a day of talk about aging . . . *our* aging:

- We need to talk about our aches and pains, stiff muscles, skin cancers, heart irregularities, how often we're getting up at night and making our way to the bathroom.
- We need to talk about our marriages. Are we doing the best we can for our wives? How are they doing?
- We need to talk about financial matters. What do each of us know that would help the others concerning taxes, philanthropy, living arrangements?
- Gloomy as the subject may be, we need to talk about dying. Why? Because we all have family members, friends, and acquaintances who are dying. What's to be learned from their experiences? How are we handling thoughts of dying?
- Maybe—most important?—we need to talk about our spiritual journeys. What's God saying to us? What do we feel called to? Any struggles? Fears? Blessings? Unresolved issues out of the past?

When the day comes, we meet. And it is a wonderful day. There are tears, laughter, surprises, great wisdom. Why not? These are my Capital-*F* Friends.

Who are my Capital-*F* Friends? Well, Gail is my first Capital-*F* Friend, but she doesn't do the "guy meetings" unless the other wives have been invited.

The rest of my Capital-*F* Friends are men:

A couple of them are thinking friends; we talk about
    ideas and questions.

A couple are my encouragement friends; we keep close
   tabs on each other.
There are my wisdom friends; we give each other
   judgment, counsel.
There is my spiritual life friend; we do a lot of talking
   about Jesus.
All of them are my fun friends: we do crazy things
   together.

I did not have Capital-*F* Friends during the first half of my life.
When people asked who my best friends were, I was content to
reply, "Gail is my best friend. I don't need anyone else."

That was the way I'd been trained to think in my younger
days. Leaders, we were told then, need to beware people who get
too close. They'll compromise your leadership magic, it was said.
They'll betray your confidences. And they may turn against you
when you least expect it. So I actually bought into that logic at one
time and kept most people at a small-*f* distance.

Then came midlife, a colossal personal failure, and the
possibility that our lives would change forever. As I took a hard
look at myself and my brokenness, a question loomed: *What do I
need more than anything else?* Answer: *a few friends.* Friends, of the
Capital-*F* brand, who will bleed for one another, speak truth to one
another, give hope to one another, trust one another, and love one
another. Convinced I was right, I started out searching for Capital-*F*
Friends.

The more I thought about the criteria for Capital-*F* Friendship,
the more I found myself thinking, *Gail and I will soon need friends
who will be there in the dying years. Not the kind of friends whose
connection is built on organizational life. Not friends who occasionally partner up for a project and then disappear. I need friends who
know my children's names, know how much money I make, know*

how to pray for me, know how to look me in the eye and say, "You're not thinking straight!"

So I set out to build a bevy of Capital-*F* Friends. Which isn't done in a short period of time. It takes time and involves a bit of risk.

When I give talks on Capital-*F* Friendships, there is one question sure to be asked. "How do you spot Capital-*F* Friends?" The follow-up question is: "When you find 'em, how do you build the friendship?"

If Gail is in the audience when a question like this is asked, she always responds, "Prayer is your first action. You ask God to give you a discerning eye about the people around you. You listen carefully for the nudge of the Holy Spirit when He says, 'There's one; there's another.' You put them on a list, pray over the list every day, and wait for the moment that heaven says, 'Go for it.'"

To which I then say, "Remember when you dated girls? Remember scanning the group of young women you knew and picking out one or two that you thought might be just right for you?"

Everyone remembers.

"Then why not go through the list of men you know—as you once did with women—and pick out one or two and 'date' them. Invite them for breakfast or lunch (and pay the bill). Ask them questions about their families, their faith, their work, their favorite pastimes. If the conversation gains energy, ask them about their family of origin. What were their fathers like? Their mothers? Happy homes or the opposite? Who were the most influential people in their younger lives? Do they enjoy their jobs? What are their hopes, dreams, and fears?

"And by the way," I add. "Observe what kinds of questions, if any, they ask you. You don't want a friendship where the other people involved don't know how or care to ask you questions about yourself.

"If you're satisfied that this is what's happening, set a date for another breakfast. Look for deepening conversations that go to the heart level. Simple as that. And if all goes well, try a third, and a fourth time to meet. In six months one of you will say to the others, 'Hey! We got a good thing going here. Let's keep doing this.'"

I do not believe that we can have ordered private worlds if we do not have Capital-F Friends. Ordering one's private world is not a one-person event. Too much of what God wants to say into our lives will be said through other people who are close (Capital-F close) to us. It is friends who will rebuke us, affirm us, advise us, and be there for us when the roof caves in.

Capital-F Friends will create an air of accountability when one is struggling with a weakness or a fear. Capital-F Friends will provide what the Quakers refer to as a clearance committee, a small group who will ask tough questions when we have a decision to make.

One of my warmest memories of my Capital-F Friends came several years ago when I had to deal with a difficult issue. I had come from a conversation with a man I greatly respect, and in the course of our talk when we disagreed over some issue, he told me that he sensed a spirit of bitterness in me.

There was hardly anything he could have said that would have stopped me faster or colder. I have feared anger and bitterness all my life because of the home I grew up in, and I thought that I handled all that in a much younger time.

"I think you have a root of bitterness in you," he'd said.

I could only respond, "I'll think about what you've said."

A day later I invited my Capital-F Friends to a breakfast and told them what had happened.

"I need help," I said. "I need for you guys to get together and talk about me behind my back. I need you to remember the times we've been together and see if you recall any time when I've shown myself in word or deed to be an angry or bitter man. Then come back and tell me what you think."

A few weeks later my Capital-*F* Friends called and suggested a lunch. Soon, after our lunch was served, one of the men said, "Gordon, we've done what you asked. We talked long and hard about what we've been seeing in you, and we want you to know that we see no root of bitterness in you. You're not an angry man. The man may have meant well, but he was wrong."

Capital-*F* Friends love one another. They flesh out the words of John, the disciple, who wrote: "This is how we know what love is: Jesus Christ [the ultimate Capital-*F* Friend] laid down his life for us. And we ought to lay down our lives for our brothers and sisters" (1 John 3:16 NIV).

Can one have Capital-*F* Friendship across the gender divide? I don't think so. There are too many regretful possibilities. But can a spouse be a Capital-*F* Friend? Possibly. Especially if you have a spouse like the one I have.

Hudson Taylor, once a great missionary leader in China, had a Capital-*F* Friend in his wife, Maria. John Pollock, one of his biographers, wrote this about them:

> Hudson would lean hard on her, drawing vigor from her spiritual maturity, her tranquility and faith. She gave him and their work all she had, every ounce of strength, every thought that crossed her intelligent mind, all the force of her love. She allowed him to drain her, and if sometimes his demands were unconsciously selfish, she was no more aware of it than he.[1]

That's not just a marriage. That's a Capital-*F* Friendship, and it is a major part of what makes an ordered private world.

Edward Farrell would not have been familiar in any way with

my Capital-*F* designation for certain friendships. Nevertheless, he clearly understood the substance of such a friendship:

> There are certain people to whom we feel we can talk because they have such a deep capacity for hearing; not hearing words only but hearing us as a person. They enable us to talk on a level which we have never before reached. They enable us to be as we have never been before. We shall never truly know ourselves unless we find people who can listen, who can enable us to emerge, to come out of ourselves, to discover who we are. We cannot discover ourselves by ourselves.[2]

Know anyone like those "certain people"? Invite them to breakfast.

FIFTEEN

REST BEYOND LEISURE
(SABBATHING)

IN THE EARLY PAGES OF THIS BOOK, I WROTE ABOUT A MOST MEMORABLE
meltdown Saturday. Soon after that day, I traveled to another city
to give an after-dinner talk to a group of businesspeople. I wanted
to speak about my recent experience and why I thought that the
"empty-soul message" I'd received that afternoon could be helpful
to others, but I was having trouble coming up with a word-picture
that might capture the audience's imagination.

When I reached my destination, my hosts took me to a private university club where I could rest before the evening's events
started. The club occupied a stately old mansion, and I took a few
moments to look around.

In my wanderings I came to a large game room. A very ornate
pool table was located at one end of the room. Approaching it, I
noted the brightly colored balls scattered across the green felt surface. There were cue-sticks in a rack on the wall nearby. There was
no one around. No signs said, "For club members only." So, I said
to myself, *why not stop for a moment and smack a few balls around
the table?*

Everyone knows that a pool game begins by collecting the

174

balls and placing them in a triangular rack. "Rack 'em up," we say. When all the balls are in place, the black 8-ball in the middle, you remove the rack. Someone goes to the other end of the table with the white cue ball and cue stick; he picks the angle of shooting that seems best. He shoots the cue ball the length of the table, and the perfect formation of balls explodes in every direction.

I did all this. Then, when the balls stopped rolling about the table, I paused because suddenly I had a vision of what had happened during my meltdown.

I saw the cue ball shattering that shape and scattering the balls to all points on the table. I saw myself coming apart in the scattering of those balls.

That was what was happening to me and others like me every day. We all wished to begin our days with the anticipation that we could stay in something like that perfect triangular shape—but life has its cue balls. They come at us from every angle, and when they hit, we are blown apart.

To press the word-picture one step further, I needed to learn how to "rack 'em up." Understand: I'm no longer talking about balls on a pool table. I'm talking about the order of one's private world. It needs to be regularly racked up.

WE NEED REST

We are a tired people. Evidence of that fatigue abounds in a multitude of articles about health problems related to overwork and exhaustion. *Stress management* and *stress relievers* are terms that are commonly used in our vocabulary now. *Workaholism* is recognized as one of the great addictions. People who would never touch a drop of alcohol can be among the most serious work addicts.

And we excuse ourselves in our over-work by telling one another that no matter how hard we are willing to work in our competitive world, there always seems to be someone willing to put in a few more hours than we are and take our job away.

What is strange about our general fatigue as a people is the fact that we are also such a leisure-oriented society. We are quite aware of the great leisure industry with its cruise ships, its fantasy resorts, and its tours to everywhere including Antarctica. The leisure industry is among the most profitable of all industries in our economy. Whole companies, organizations, and retail chain stores are committed to providing the clothing and equipment with which people can pursue fun and good times.

We probably have more time for leisure than we ever had before. The five-day workweek is, after all, a relatively new innovation in history; we have moved away from the farm, where there was always more work to do; we can leave work behind if we want and head for leisure. So why is there so much exhaustion and fatigue today? Is it real? Imagined? Or is the contemporary form of exhaustion evidence that we no longer understand genuine rest, which is different from the pursuit of leisure?

There is a biblical view of rest that needs to be uncovered and examined. In fact, the Bible reveals God Himself to be the first "rester." "On the seventh day he rested" (Gen. 2:2 NIV). An even more enlightening comment is made by Moses in Exodus 31:17: "In six days the LORD made heaven and earth, but on the seventh day He ceased from labor, and was refreshed." The literal translation suggests the phrase "He refreshed Himself."

Does God indeed need to rest? Of course not! But did God choose to rest? Yes. Why? Because God subjected creation to a rhythm of work and rest that He revealed by observing the rhythm Himself, as a precedent for everyone else. In this way, He showed us a key to order in our private worlds.

This rest was not meant to be a luxury, but rather a *necessity* for those who want to have growth and maturity. Since we have not understood that rest is a necessity, we have perverted its meaning, substituting for the rest that God first demonstrated things called leisure or amusement. These do not bring any order at all to the private world. Leisure and amusement may be enjoyable, but they are to the private world of the individual like cotton candy to the digestive system. They provide a momentary lift, but they will not last.

I am not by any means critical of the pursuit of fun-filled moments, diversion, laughter, or recreation. I am proposing that these alone will not restore the soul in the way that we crave. Although they may provide a sort of momentary rest for the body, they will not satisfy the deep need for rest within the private world.

Years ago there was a famous ad campaign for a liniment, which promised that the product would penetrate deeply into sore muscles, bringing relief from aches and pains. Sabbath rest penetrates to the deepest levels of fatigue in the inner, private world. This fatigue is rarely touched by any of the modern amusements.

THE MEANING OF SABBATH REST

Closing the Loop

When God rested, He looked on His work, enjoyed its completed appearance, and then reflected on its meaning: "And God saw that it was good" (Gen. 1:10). This shows us the first of the three principles of genuine rest. God gave His work meaning and acknowledged its completion. In so doing, He taught us that there is a necessary exercise of appreciation and dedication for our routines.

Hi-tech systems planners like to use the phrase "closing the loop" to describe the completion of a phase in an electrical circuit. They also use the phrase when they want to say that a task has been completed or every person in a project has been informed or consulted.

So you could say that on the seventh day, God closed the loop on His primary creation activity. He closed it by resting and looking back on it to survey what had been accomplished.

This rest then is, first of all, a time of looking backward, of loop-closing. We gaze on our work and ask questions like: What does my work mean? For whom did I do this work? How well was the work done? Why did I do this? What results did I expect, and what did I receive?

To put it another way, the rest God instituted was meant first and foremost to cause us to interpret our work, to press meaning into it, to make sure we know to whom it is properly dedicated.

Brother Lawrence was a cook in a monastery. He learned to press meaning into virtually every action of his day. Note his capacity to see not only meaning but also purpose in his labor:

> I turn my little omelet in the pan for the love of God. When it is finished, if I have nothing to do, I prostrate myself on the ground and worship my God, who gave me this grace to make it, after which I arise happier than a king. When I can do nothing else, it is enough to have picked up a straw for the love of God. People look for ways of learning how to love God. They hope to attain it by I know not how many different practices. They take much trouble to abide in His presence by varied means. Is it not a shorter and more direct way to do everything for the love of God, to make use of all the tasks one's lot in life demands to show him that love, and to maintain his presence within by the communion of our heart with his? There is nothing complicated about it. One has only to turn to it honestly and simply.[1]

I am sure that most of us desire periods of time like that. The average worker has a desperate need to feel that his or her work means something, has significance, and is appreciated. But while we crave that assurance, we do not see the importance of taking time to gain it. A busyness, a frantic pace, sets in, and we delay our quests for meaning and interpretation; before long we have learned to get along without them. We lose sight of the question, "What's this all for?" We become content to allow the meaning and value of our work to be computed merely in the amount on our paychecks. Few people appreciate how dry and barren this leaves our private worlds.

Returning to the Eternal Truths

There is a second way biblical rest restores order to the private world. True rest is happening when we pause regularly amid daily routines to sort out the truths and commitments by which we are living.

We are daily the objects of a bombardment of messages competing for our loyalties and labors. We are pushed and pulled in a thousand different directions, asked to make decisions and value judgments, to invest our resources and our time. By what standard of truth do we make these decisions?

God meant for His people to take a day each week in which this question was firmly dealt with. And, in fact, He caused them to set aside a series of annual feast days during which major themes of eternal truth and divine action could be recalled and celebrated. You could call it a recalibration of the spirit.

Separating out the truths that are central to life is essential when one remembers that, according to Jeremiah, the heart is deceitful. We are vulnerable at all times to distortions of the truth, to persuasions that the true is really false and the false really true. Remember the words of the hymn writer:

> *Prone to wander, Lord, I feel it,*
> *Prone to leave the God I love.*[2]

The hymn reflects on the inexorable inward drift that must be regularly checked by measuring our thoughts and values against the eternal truths that have been revealed through the Scripture and the mighty acts of God.

The Jewish theologian Abraham Joshua Heschel looked at rest in the Sabbath tradition and wrote,

> The meaning of the Sabbath is to celebrate time rather than space. Six days a week, we live under the tyranny of things of space; on the Sabbath we try to become attuned to holiness in time. It is a day on which we are called upon to share what is eternal in time, to turn from the results of creation to the mystery of creation; from the world of creation to the creation of the world.[3]

We need to ask ourselves: Is this happening in my own private world?

The clapboards of our New Hampshire home expand and contract in response to temperature extremes. The result is that some nails work loose and have to be pounded back in to regain a snug hold. This "repounding" is what happens during a genuine rest period, be it in the privacy of that quiet day or in the midst of a congregation while we worship the living God.

One of the great joys of repeating the traditional creeds of the Christian church is that it gives us an opportunity to reaffirm the central truths of God's revelation. As we say, "I believe," we begin to hammer back the nails of our convictions and commitments. And we separate those beliefs out from what we choose not to believe.

The same thing happens when we sing grand old hymns and pray certain prayers. The nails are being pounded back in, and order is being restored to a drifting spirit in our private worlds.

Reaffirmations occur on that special rest day, if we take time in private for reading, meditating, and reflecting.

My wife shared with me an entry in her journal on this very subject:

> A glorious Lord's Day. Have been reading at length about the Sabbath. Feel more and more strongly that I've not fully utilized God's command to rest.
>
> It's not a rule that restricts but it is a rule that liberates. For He made me to need rest. And physically and mentally we are freed to better performance if we live within His "design specifications." And it is a day of reminding us who God is. Every seventh day I need to come back to the fixed Center.
>
> Don Stephenson remarked today that for him and others Sunday is just that—a day to come back to the straight edge and be encouraged to go back to the "mire."

I would propose that we need to ask hard questions, both of ourselves and of our churches, concerning whether the sort of rest that reaffirms truth is actually happening. It is possible for Christ-followers and their churches to become so busy carrying on programs—for whatever good purpose—that the worship-rest necessary to the private world never happens.

Thus, rest is not only a looking back at the meaning of my work and the path I have so recently walked in my life, but it is also a refreshing of my belief and commitment to Christ. It is a fine tuning of my inner navigational instruments so that I can make my way through the world for another week.

Defining Our Mission

If the first two meanings centered on what was past and present, this one centers on the future. When we rest in the biblical sense, we affirm our intentions to pursue a Christ-centered tomor-row. We ponder where we are headed in the coming week, month, or year. We define our intentions and make our dedications.

General George Patton demanded that his men know and be able to articulate exactly what the current mission was. "What is your mission?" he would frequently ask. The definition of the mission was the most important piece of information a soldier could carry into combat. Based on that knowledge, he could make his decisions and implement the plan. That is exactly what hap-pens when I pursue biblical rest. I take a hard look at my mission. And it has taught me to make a small pause even in my spiritual disciplines each morning to ask the question, "What is my mis-sion today?" Not to regularly ask this question is to leave yourself open to mistakes of judgment and direction.

Jesus often withdrew to seek solitude. While others were lulled to the rest of sleep, Jesus was drawn to the rest of gaining strength and direction for His next phase of mission. No wonder He met every encounter with a fresh burst of wisdom. No wonder He had ample courage not to fight back, not to defend Himself. His spirit was always rested, His private world ordered. Without this kind of rest, our private worlds will always be strained and disordered.

There is an easily neglected story recorded in two of the New Testament Gospels. I would not rank it among the top ten stories of Jesus, but it has been a very instructive bit of Scripture for me over the years. I return to it often whenever I need to be reminded of the importance of the filled, the *racked up* soul.

Jesus had spent a Sabbath day (Saturday) in the village—His favorite village?—of Capernaum (in Galilee). During the morn-ing, He lectured in the synagogue and healed people. Then He retreated to the home of Simon Peter and Andrew, two of His ear-liest disciples. Word must have spread as to where He could be found because at sundown, the official end of the Sabbath, a crowd gathered demanding that Jesus heal the sick and purge the demon-possessed. Late into the evening, the Lord responded to everyone who approached Him.

For Jesus, that day had to have been exhausting both physically and spiritually. Talk about a drain on one's body and soul. Talk about ideal conditions for one to succumb to a meltdown experience.

The next morning, Mark wrote, Jesus was up and out of the house before anyone else, on His way to a "solitary place" where He prayed. Now, I've read those words more than a few times, but it was only after my own sinkhole day that I came to appreciate what I was reading. I saw that Jesus knew how long He could mix it up with crowds before He had to retreat to a quiet spot and tend to the private-world work of "sabbathing."

Sabbathing. Did anyone pick up my changing the word *sabbath* from a noun to a verb?

To Sabbath: this is the first step in the life of one who seeks to bring order to his or her private world. One fills the soul when he *sabbaths.* Most of us recognize the word *Sabbath* as referring to the seventh day of the week, a day set aside for rest from work and the hassle of regular life. I have taken the liberty of stretching the word to speak of any time, on any day, when one suspends his work and connects with the Father in heaven.

It appears that Jesus remained in His solitary place for a considerable amount of time. Doing what? Again, my answer: *sabbathing.* Let me imagine what He did. Rested, might have even dozed a bit, reflected on the activities of previous days, recalled blessed moments and gave thanks for them, worshiped, recalled (and sang) Old Testament Scriptures, prayed, listened for the words of His Father, reaffirmed His sense of mission, made decisions about what should come next. Maybe—since the Bible says that Jesus was present at Creation—He was admiring some of His own created beauty.

Then the inevitable moment came when His reverie was

interrupted by His disciples who'd been searching for Him. Again, I'm using my imagination to fill in the blanks of this story when I speculate that Jesus had deliberately kept this solitary location a secret, *even from His friends*. That might explain why they had to search for Him.

Finding Him, the disciples immediately pressed Him to scramble back into yesterday's activities: to return to Capernaum because—as they put it—"everyone (meaning last night's crowd) is looking for you."

Everyone is looking for you. *Everyone!* I've thought about this many times. If you're launching a movement—and Jesus was— the report that a crowd is clamoring to get more of you should be very good news. It means that your "favorables" are surging. The disciples weren't dumb (not always, anyway); they knew that Jesus needed exposure, to be out there where everyone could come under His spell as they had.

But the disciples' plan was not in alignment with Jesus' think- ing. After all, He'd been the one *sabbathing*, not them. And this is huge; it explains what happens next.

The disciples wanted him back in Capernaum, but Jesus re- sponded to the disciples' idea with a blunt no, saying, "I have other towns and villages to go to."

May I be frank at this point? Had I been in Jesus' sandals, I would have caved to the disciples' wishes and returned to Capernaum. *Heaven must be in this*, I can hear myself reasoning. Five simple words would have convinced me: *Everyone is looking for you*. Everyone! I like *everyone*.

But Jesus wasn't buying this "everyone" criteria, as some of us might. Instead He said, "I have other places to go."

Here's the place that this story becomes so important to me. Why, I ask, was Jesus so confident that He was right and the disciples wrong?

My answer? Jesus' decision was sabbath-produced; He'd spent time, alone and quiet, in that hidden place. You could say that He'd been in conversation with His heavenly Father and that His mission in the world (the son of Man has come to seek and save lost people; Luke 19:10) had been reaffirmed between them.

Jesus' logic—to turn away from the crowd and toward other towns and villages—is not the kind of decision most politicians and entertainers would make. But it is the logic of heaven. Having sabbathed, Jesus could think clearly, make wise judgments, and stand firm in His convictions even when He was in the minority.

I have searched the Scriptures for other examples of similarly ordered people who understood that living a sound and sturdy life begins with sabbathing.

Moses, during a high-stress moment in his leadership, does the "rack 'em up" thing in what was called the "Tent of Meeting," where, it is said, he conversed with God "face to face, as one speaks to a friend" (Ex. 33:11 NIV). He seems interested in three things:

1. God's purposes for Israel,
2. Whether God will be present with the people as they travel, and
3. If God's power (glory) can be counted on when times get tough.

Did Jesus pose similar questions when He was out on that hillside alone? If you believe in the humanity of Jesus (as well as His divinity), this is not a dumb question.

Daniel was a worshiper of Israel's God when he served in three successive administrations of despotic kings. How did he keep himself spiritually oriented? It sounds like the secret was in his daily mini-sabbathing routines.

The man found a way to interrupt each workday with three

regular "rack 'em up" sabbath experiences. His chosen solitary place sounds like an apartment with a window that opened toward Jerusalem.

Why would he have done this?

Ask yourself what it must have been like to work under a pagan king and to have to participate in a government that was evil. Every day must have brought consultations and decisions that required enormous wisdom and discretion. No wonder he wanted to kneel in the direction of Jerusalem. It was the only recourse for one who wanted to keep his soul open and hospitable to the presence of Israel's God.

Daniel's sabbathing routine partially explains these words: "They [his enemies] could find no corruption in him, because he was trustworthy and neither corrupt nor negligent" (Dan. 6:4 NIV).

Mary, the soon-to-be mother of Jesus sought the "rack 'em up" sabbathing quietness of the countryside and the company of the aging Elizabeth (herself miraculously pregnant) after an angel's announcement that she was to be the mother of the Messiah. She saw in Elizabeth the sturdiness of an older woman who could walk her through the process of obeying heaven's call. When it was time for her to return to Nazareth for the birth of her son, she was prepared, emboldened to face that great moment. Clearly, her private world was in order.

CHOOSING TO REST

One of the noted vicars of the Church of England was Charles Simeon, of Holy Trinity Church in Cambridge. For more than fifty years he preached from its pulpit, and the people crowded the sanctuary, standing in the aisles to hear him.

Simeon was a fellow at Kings College, and he lived in apartments that overlooked the courtyard in the college complex. His second-floor dwellings provided him an exclusive opening out to the roof where he would often walk, one of his physical forms of rest, while he talked with God. That rooftop became known as Simeon's walk.

A busy and brilliant man, Simeon was in touch with students at the colleges in Cambridge, with a large congregation, and with church and missionary leaders around the world. He wrote (in longhand) literally thousands of letters, edited fifty books of his own sermons, and served as one of the founders of several major missionary organizations. But he never ceased to find time for the rest that his private world demanded.

A sample of his private exercises can be found in this entry to his journal, recorded by Hugh Hopkins, a Simeon biographer.

> I spent this day as I have for these 43 last years, as a day of humiliation; having increased need of such season every year I live.

Hopkins wrote,

> Self-humiliation for Charles Simeon consisted not of belittling the gifts that God had given him or pretending that he was a man of no account, or exaggerating the sins of which he was very conscious. He went about it by consciously bringing himself into the presence of God, dwelling thoughtfully on his majesty and glory, magnifying the mercy of his forgiveness and the wonder of his love. These were the things that humbled him—not so much his own sinfulness but God's incredible love.[4]

Simeon enjoyed a lifelong effectiveness under enormous strain. I have no doubt that a large part of his secret of endurance was his deliberate and disciplined pursuit of sabbath rest.

For the Jew, the Sabbath was, first of all, a day. A day set aside in obedience to God. The law forbade work of any kind, allowing only the sort of observances such as we have already reviewed. Christ-followers have little idea of how special the Sabbath was to pious Jews. We would do well to listen and hear what they think. An Israeli tourist brochure tells us that one rabbi wrote of Sabbath,

> Make the Sabbath an eternal monument of the knowledge and sanctification of God, both in the center of your busy public life and in the peaceful retreat of your domestic hearth. For six days cultivate the earth and rule it. . . . But the seventh is the Sabbath of the Lord thy God. . . . Let [a man] therefore realize that the Creator of old is the living God of today, [that He] watches every man and every human effort, to see how man uses or abuses the world loaned to him and the forces bestowed upon him, and that He is the sole architect to Whom every man has to render an account of his week's labors.

What is important behind these statements is the Jewish awareness of a unique pace to Sabbath. Routines are to stop; labor is to cease. Even the homemaker in the pious Jewish family is to refrain from cooking or menial tasks. Food is prepared before Sabbath begins so that she also can enjoy the fruit of the special rest day. This is a far cry from the incredible, filled-up, pressurized day many Christ-followers tend to make of their "day of rest."

In our Christian tradition we have chosen to make that day not the seventh—as Jews, as well as some within the body of Christ, observe, in obeying the commandment—but the first day of the week, in recognition of the resurrection of Christ. But having made that choice, what have we done with *our* day—this time that God gave as a special gift?

A man with whom I once worshiped every week said to me

after one particularly long Sunday of church activity, "I'm sure glad that there is only one rest day per week. I'd burn out if we had to go through two 'days of rest' like this every seven days."

His humor conveys a serious charge against many Christian leaders and churches who have turned Sunday into a day of unrest and, perhaps for some, the most tension-filled day of the week.

But Sabbath is more than just a day. It is a principle of rest along the lines of the three dimensions I have already mentioned. And what might happen should we choose the peace of Sabbath rest rather than the fun of secular leisure?

First, Sabbath rest means worship with the believing family. In proper worship we will have a chance to exercise all three aspects that lead to the rest of our private worlds: looking backward, upward, and ahead. Such worship is non-negotiable to the person committed to walking with God.

I am moved by the words of Luke, who described the Sabbath discipline of Jesus: "And He came to Nazareth, where He had been brought up; *and as was His custom, He entered the synagogue on the Sabbath*" (Luke 4:16). One never sees Christ slipping away from the public worship of the Father.

But second, Sabbath means a deliberate acceptance of personal rest and tranquility within the individual life. Sabbath means a rest that brings peace into the private world. As Christ pressed stillness into a storm, order into the being of a demon-possessed maniac, health into a desperately sick woman, and life into a dead friend, so He seeks to press peace into the harried private world of the man or woman who has been in the marketplace all week. But there is a condition. We must accept this peace as a gift and take the time to receive it.

As a pastor, I have long felt that Sunday was anything but Sabbath rest for my wife and me. It was many years into my Christ-following adulthood before I realized that I had been robbing myself of a necessary form of restoration. The fact was that I needed some sort of sabbath for my own private world, and I wasn't getting it. When I looked at my Sundays, it seemed impossible to think that I would ever enjoy Sabbath's rejuvenating gift. How could I preach three Sunday morning sermons and a frequent evening sermon, as well as be available throughout the day to the people of my congregation, and expect to be restored? Rarely did a Sunday end without Gail and me being on the verge of exhaustion. Day of rest indeed!

Many years ago I took a four-month sabbatical leave of absence from my work. Rather than go off to a university to study, I chose to go to New Hampshire, where we built Peace Ledge. The outstanding experience of those four months was the silence and peace we discovered on Sundays.

Although I enjoyed the construction of Peace Ledge immensely, I promised myself that I would do no work on the Lord's Day. Thus, when Sunday came, we spent a few early morning hours reading, thinking, and praying. And then we went to a local church where we could worship. We did not know many of the people, but we tried to throw ourselves into the worship and draw from the prayers, the hymns, and the sermon food for our spirits. We made it a time of affirming our convictions, thanking God for blessings, and committing ourselves to the coming week in which we would try to reflect the honor of the Lord.

Our Sunday afternoons during those four months were quiet hours for walks in the woods, deep conversations and a searching process as we evaluated our spiritual disciplines and progress in Christ-likeness. It was a marvelously restful sabbath experience for us; I had never known what it could be like before that time.

We were hooked on sabbaths when we returned from our sabbatical. But suddenly it was back to sermons, and counseling, and programming. Business as usual on Sunday. We felt robbed. And so it was that we decided our sabbath would be another day of the week. We were not going to miss God's gift. On Sundays, we would try to help others enjoy their sabbaths. But for us, the peace normally reserved for that day would have to happen at some other time. And that was fine.

Sabbath for Gail and me became Thursday. To the extent that we could achieve it, we budgeted that day of the week for rest in our private worlds. It meant total withdrawal from our congregation whenever possible, even laying aside the routines of our home if we could. We learned that if we were going to be useful to those associated with us in ministry, to our children, and to the congregation, we would have to jealously guard this opportunity for spiritual restoration.

There is no legalism here—rather a freedom to accept a gift. Frankly, I think some have destroyed the joy of Sabbath, as did the Pharisees, by surrounding it with prescriptive laws and precedents. That is not our Sabbath. Our Sabbath was made for us, given to us by God. Its purpose is worship and restoration, and whatever it takes to make that happen, we will do.

It is important to say that we probably could not have pursued sabbath rest as easily when our children were young and needed more constant attention. And it is also important to say, as Gail often observes, that we do our people a favor by withdrawing from them for rest. For when we return, we have something to offer that God probably could not have given us in any other atmosphere.

Obviously, every Thursday could not be budgeted for sabbath.

But we discovered that if we made a regular attempt at such a discipline, the results were tremendous. Our private worlds were indeed substantially reordered. The most astounding discovery was that I felt not only rested but also able to use the times of other days in a far more effective fashion.

What had happened, much to my amazement, was that by bringing this restful order to my private world through proper sabbath observance, I was able to impact my public world in the days that followed with much greater wisdom and judgment.

I believe that sabbath rest may mean a day a week. But it can happen at any time, in large and small doses, when we choose to set aside an hour or more for the pursuit of intimacy with God. All of us need a "Simeon's walk."

But let me be quick to underscore that this rest, which is sabbathlike, ought to be a fixed allocation in the budgeting of our time. We do not rest because our work is done; we rest because God commanded it and created us to have a need for it.

That is important to think about because our current view of rest and leisure denies that principle. Most of us think of resting as something we do *after* our work is done. But sabbath is not something that happens after. It may, in fact, be something that is pursued *before*. If we assume that this rest comes only after work is complete, many of us are in trouble, for we have jobs where the work is never finished. And that in part is why some of us rarely rest; never finishing our work, no time for sabbath peace and restoration.

I had to learn to pursue sabbath rest without a sense of guilt. I had to realize that there was nothing wrong with laying aside other work for the purpose of enjoying God's gift of special time. Thus, sabbaths have gone into our calendars with regularity. They are planned weeks in advance, along with other priorities. And when someone has proposed a supper, a ball game, or a committee meeting on a day set aside for the reordering of our private worlds, my wife and I have simply said, "Sorry, we have a commitment on that day. It's sabbath for us."

The world and the church need genuinely *rested* Christfollowers: Christians who are regularly refreshed by true Sabbath rest, not just leisure or time off. When a godly rest is achieved, you will see just how tough and resilient believers can actually be.

Whether it's Jesus in that solitary place or Moses in his tent,

Daniel at his window, or Mary at Elizabeth's home, you get the impression that these "rack 'em up" sabbathing moments of withdrawal were marked with a beautiful communion between heaven and earth that relatively few in each generation know about.

More than two hundred years ago, the notable William Wilberforce, member of the British Parliament, faced a career-altering opportunity. It was rumored in the press that he was being considered for a cabinet position under the new prime minister, Lord Addington.

Biographers say that Wilberforce struggled with this possibility. Such an appointment would have sent him nearly to the top of His Majesty's government, but he had long ago established an intention to lead the antislavery movement in England. A cabinet position would have scuttled that effort.

Some days into this personal battle, Wilberforce awakened to a day of choice-making: a sabbath day. At some point during that day while in a solitary place, the man wrote these words in his journal: "Blessed be God for this day of rest and religious occupation, wherein *earthly things assume their true size and comparative insignificance; ambition is stunted*, and I hope my affections in some degree rise to things above."[5]

I have no idea what William Wilberforce did that day to reach the conclusion that he would not join the prime minister's cabinet. But I have this feeling that if there had been no sabbathing, the Wilberforce story might have ended up quite differently.

Wilberforce never joined the cabinet, but he did go on to lead England into one of its greatest political and economic decisions: to get out of the slavery business.

Oh, almost no one but the historians know anything about Lord Addington or those who did join his government. But millions of people know about William Wilberforce and his contribution to Western civilization. That's what sabbathing can accomplish.

ORDERING YOUR PRIVATE WORLD

So that's what happened to Jesus because He *sabbathed* one morning on a hillside. His private world (to use Wilberforce's words) assumed its true size. He knew when to say no and when to say yes.

When I gave my talk to the businesspeople that evening, I started with my experience at the pool table. You could tell that a lot of them got the point.

COURAGE, APPRECIATION, DEPTH

IN MY SENIOR YEAR AT THE STONY BROOK SCHOOL, I WAS REQUIRED TO take a course called Senior Bible, taught by the very well-known scholar and theologian (as well as classical pianist and mountain climber) Dr. Frank E. Gabelein. It was Dr. Gabelein's concern that we senior boys be as prepared spiritually for college as possible. The class he taught was one of the most difficult I ever experienced.

Among other things, Dr. Gabelein believed in Scripture memorization. Thus, over the course of the school year we were required to memorize (I'm guessing) about two hundred verses and paragraphs of Scripture. What's more, Dr. Gabelein reserved the right to approach any of us on campus at any time and ask us to quote this verse or that one.

When we had to write out these verses during tests, it was understood that we would write the verse not only word for word as it was found in the King James Bible but also with perfect capitalization, punctuation, and spelling.

Had you been on campus in those days, you would have quickly recognized we seniors. Each of us had a pocket full of index cards with Bible verses, which we rehearsed constantly.

Practicing a verse sounded like this: "(Capital G) God is our refuge and strength (comma), an ever-present help in trouble (period). (Capital *T*) Therefore we will not fear (comma), though the earth give way and the mountains fall into the heart of the sea (comma), though its waters roar and foam and the mountains quake with their surging (period)."[1]

I would be dishonest if I did not admit that almost all of us students resented this discipline deeply. But Dr. Gabelein never apologized for his insistence that we store Scripture into our private worlds.

Now, advance the calendar sixty years.

I have begun to experience a small unsteadiness when I am walking. Especially in the dark at night: there is this tiny sensation of wobbliness. Also, about this same time, my hearing is beginning to degrade.

I visited my doctor twice about these irregularities, and he waved them off as symptoms of old age. "Gordon, you're seventy-four years old," he said. "Your body is simply getting old."

When I made a third visit, he finally agreed that I should have an MRI. The next morning I was first in line at the hospital for my MRI. Two hours later my doctor phoned our home—something he's never done before—and said, "Gordon, I don't want you to worry, but I have to tell you that the MRI people found a tumor about the size of an egg on the edge of your brain. It's going to have to come out."

A tumor! On the brain! Scary. As I took in these words, I remained quiet for a few seconds, trying to think of an appropriate response to my doctor's words. And then from somewhere in my mind leapt up this thought:

(Capital G) God is our refuge and strength (comma), an ever-present help in trouble (period). (Capital T) Therefore we will not fear . . . I will not fear . . . I will not fear . . . (period, period, period).

Dr. Gabelein knew exactly what he was doing sixty years ago. He was planting the seeds of faith and Scripture into the hearts and minds of his young students. He knew that there would come days filled with tumors, losses, failures, conflicts, fears, betrayals, exhaustions . . . and a whole lot more.

Soon the surgery to remove that tumor was scheduled. It would take seven hours, Gail and I were told. Fourteen people would make up the team in the OR. In the first forty-eight hours after the surgery, almost three dozen people would march in and out of my life helping my body recover its strength.

In preparation I asked God to keep my private world in order by giving me three words of clarity. A day or two before the surgery the words came. They seemed to slide into my heart and become operational immediately.

The words were: *Courage, Appreciation, Depth.*

Courage: to face the unknown and leave it in heaven's hands.

Appreciation: to make sure that every person who crossed my path (whether surgeons, nurses, students, or food, janitorial, and administrative personnel) heard a word or received a note of thanks from me.

Depth: that my attitudes and behavior would project the spirit of Christ; that my experiences would show me more of the purposes of God.

That's a bit of an idea how a private world works.

STUDY GUIDE

BY LESLIE H. STOBBLE

WORKING THROUGH A STUDY GUIDE ABOUT ORDERING OUR PRIVATE worlds may seem a peculiarly atavistic response to a call for more inner-directed living. Yet most of us need something to help us develop a more disciplined approach to ordering our private worlds as believers.

The author found that one practical way to learn to listen to God speak was to keep a journal. With pencil in hand ready to write, he found that there was an expectancy, a readiness to hear anything God might wish to whisper through his reading and reflection.

We hope this study guide will aid the reader in establishing reflective writing as a habit. Some questions are designed to get you to think through the implications of the author's suggestions and to write down your responses. Others we hope will trigger life responses. Questions with an asterisk (*) have been inserted to facilitate discussion in group settings.

PREFACE: THE DAY I HIT THE WALL

1. What experience or insight triggered your desire to read *Ordering Your Private World*?

2. What enemy (or enemies) to bringing order to your private world do you need to identify?

3. Who is your most persistent advocate of ordering your private world? Compare Ephesians 1:13 with John 14:26.

4. List the five sectors of your private world that need ordering.

a. _____

b. _____

c. _____

d. _____

e. _____

Now rate yourself on a scale of 1–10 for each category, with ten representing perfection.

*5. What biographies have motivated you to move toward a more ordered inner life? What made these persons so influential?

CHAPTER 1: THE SINKHOLE SYNDROME

1. In what ways has your life during the past year illustrated the author's words: "Our outer, or public, world is easier to deal with. It is much more measurable, visible, and expandable"?

*2. What might be described as a "sinkhole experience" in your life?

3. The author writes that the private world "is a center in which choices and values can be determined, where

solitude and reflection might be pursued." What else can happen there, according to the author?

*4. Which public worlds are screaming for your attention? Put an asterisk beside the ones to which you've capitulated.

_____

_____

_____

_____

5. What are some fears that may have prevented your seeking the inner peace that comes alongside a well-ordered inner world?

*6. Looking ahead, can you think of an event or pressure that could become powerful enough to become a sinkhole in your life?

*7. Read Ephesians 3:14–21. What connection do you see between verse 20 and verse 16?

CHAPTER 2: A VIEW FROM THE BRIDGE

1. Read the story of the submarine captain at the beginning of this chapter. Now compare this with the "bridge" appearance described in Acts 27:21–25. What can we learn from the apostle Paul's expression of confidence?

2. If you were a Christian counselor and a Jerald H. Maxwell came to you, what would you tell him, based on Jesus' response to the disciples in the storm on the Sea of Galilee?

*3. Where do we need to build up resources to be able to withstand the steadily mounting pressures of the world around us? See Romans 12:2.

4. What set Mary Slessor apart from the others of her generation?

*5. From your circle of friends and people you have read about, who would be your best contemporary model of inner orderliness? Why?

*6. What are the two most important choices you can make to gain this kind of inner "bridge"?

a. _____

b. _____

CHAPTER 3: CAUGHT IN A GOLDEN CAGE

1. Examine Gordon's discussion of *drivenness* and its accompanying symptoms. Do you recognize any of these in your life, or in the life of someone close to you?

2. Make an attempt to sort out and catalogue the motives that energize you as an involved Christian. Take time to listen to the quiet voice of the Holy Spirit and begin to write.

3. What are some of the negative components of stress in your life today?

_____

_____

_____

_____

*4. List the stresses the apostle Paul experienced in his life of ministry as described in 2 Corinthians 11:24–28. Reflect on them by comparing them with the negative components of stress that you listed for the preceding question.

_____

_____

_____

_____

_____

_____

5. How did Paul gain the inner resilience needed for his stress level? Using a concordance, isolate the words *pray* and *prayer* in the apostle's letter for the inner ordering of his world.

6. Having listed the characteristics of the driven person that are obvious in your life, ask a friend or a spouse to pinpoint those characteristics in your life.

*7. With what three assets had God blessed Saul at the time he became king? What advantage did they gain him?

a. _____

b. _____

c. _____

8. As you read the account of Saul's experience, write down the parallels in your own life.

_____

_____

_____

_____

9. Now lay these before the Lord, asking Him for insight into action you can take to get out of the golden cage. List action points below as they come to you.

_____

_____

_____

_____

*10. How can we help Christian leaders trapped by the golden-cage syndrome?

CHAPTER 4: THE TRAGIC TALE OF A SUCCESSFUL LOSER

1. Reflecting on the chapter-opening story of the man with the boat, examine experiences during your formative years that may have shaped your present attitudes. Describe each with a one-sentence statement that pinpoints the key issue. If they were positive, take time to thank God for each one.

*2. Make a two-column chart. In the first column, list the external goals of the driven person, and in the second column, list the parallels you recognize in your life.

*3. List the motivational basis for people you know who may be driven.

_____

_____

_____

_____

_____

_____

4. Which of these motivational mainsprings shape your inner world? Describe how they affect your actions.

5. What experiences does the author consider critical to changing the lifestyle of the driven person?

*6. Identify the key elements in Peter's interaction with Jesus that produced change. Consider Matthew 14:25–30; 16:13–17; 26:31–35; and John 21:15–22, among others.

7. Whom do you need to forgive in order to combat the drivenness in your life? Do you believe that forgiveness will relieve you? What action will you take to gain the release that forgiveness can give you?

*8. Do all of us have to experience a classic confrontation with Jesus as Paul did before we can change from being driven persons to called persons? If so, why? If not, why not?

204

CHAPTER 5: LIVING AS A CALLED PERSON

1. Return to the author's memory of the round table in the train yard. Has God ever round-tabled you?

2. According to the author, what is the difference between a driven person and a called person? Have you ever recognized someone else living out his or her calling?

*3. How did the disciples of Jesus match the apostle Paul's description of the called in 1 Corinthians 1:26–31?

4. Where do we see the difference between John the Baptist and King Saul most vividly?

*5. What are the characteristics of the called person, according to the author?

6. If you were to measure yourself according to those characteristics, what is your weakest link? Set aside a specific time to be before the Lord and let the Holy Spirit do His gracious work in you. Either make a journal entry or record your experience here.

_____

_____

_____

_____

_____

_____

7. What do you sense is *your* primary purpose as a Christian servant?

8. Write out your "desert" experience. If you cannot identify one, plan for a specific time when you can be alone with God and settle your purpose and priorities. Then write them out.

*9. Describe two or more life situations in which the lessons John learned in the desert would help you in today's environment.

10. The author asks, "What makes you tick? Why are you doing all of that? What do you hope to gain as a result? And what would be your reaction if it was all taken away?" Write out your answers after you have had time to reflect on the questions.

CHAPTER 6: HAS ANYONE SEEN MY TIME? I'VE MISPLACED IT!

1. How do you respond to each of the following statements?
   a. My desk has a cluttered appearance.
   b. I am aware of a diminution in my self-esteem.
   c. There are a series of forgotten appointments, telephone messages to which I have failed to respond, and deadlines I have begun to miss.
   d. I tend to invest my energies in unproductive tasks.
   e. I do not feel good about the quality of my work.
   f. I do not experience intimacy with God on a regular basis.
   g. My personal relationships are suffering.
   h. I really don't like myself, my job, or much of anything else.

2. None of us can affect improvement in too many areas at the same time. We need about three weeks to break a

habit and another three to feel comfortable with a new one. So set your sight on changing the area that you consider most critical at this time in your ordering of your private world. Then mark on your calendar when you will focus on the second area. Below, note the two areas you have selected for improvement.

a. _____

b. _____

*3. In the beginning, to budget time effectively, you must establish priorities within the framework of your life calling. How does Jesus illustrate this in Luke 18, as He sets out for Jerusalem?

4. What do you consider your number one mission in life? In what way does it (should it) inform your time schedule?

5. Jesus understood His limits, says the author. In what ways could you be exceeding the natural limits God has given you for your life?

*6. Moses had forty years in the wilderness; David, his years of exile from the court of Saul; Jesus, thirty years to begin His ministry. Describe what you could consider a similar, usually unexplainable delay in getting on with your mission in life. Can you list discernible benefits from that time?

7. Jesus invested His life in twelve disciples. In whom are you investing your life as a parent, as a businessperson, as a leader in your church, as a professional? What are you trying to achieve in your discipling role?

*8. What can you do to multiply your ministry as Jesus did?

CHAPTER 7: RECAPTURING MY TIME

1. Complete the following sentence: I am least effective in managing my time in my (describe sphere of activity) . . .

*2. Check the validity of MacDonald's four laws of unseized time based on your experiences. Copy each law and then describe one situation where that law has been in operation in your life.

   a. _____

   b. _____

   c. _____

   d. _____

3. List two of your tasks that you could pass on to your spouse, associate, lay leader (if you are a pastor), secretary, son, or daughter without detracting from what you do best. (This may be a task you really enjoy doing but one you know is not central to your life mission.)

   a. _____

   b. _____

   If you are in a group, allow some of the group members to share their lists.

4. Suggest why the "strong people" in your life rob you of valuable time you could give to your family.

5. What are you doing for the sake of public acclaim? You may need to work out this answer before the Lord in a special time with Him.

6. What would happen if you were to implement John 9:4 in your life?

7. Is there anything in your life about which you feel as strongly as Jesus did about going to Jerusalem, as recorded in Matthew 16:21?

8. Analyze your life rhythms. When are you most effective? What can you do to match your most effective moments with your most significant tasks?

*9. List the criteria you can use to distinguish the good from the best for you in light of your responsibilities.

_____

_____

_____

_____

10. What portions of your day/week should you be budgeting far in advance so you can fend off intruders?

*11. What were Jesus' time priorities according to these passages: Luke 4:16; 4:42–43; 5:27; 6:12; 9:21–22; 18:16; 19:5?

CHAPTER 8: THE BETTER MAN LOST

*1. What is the greatest danger of flabby thinking in a church or society? If there is a specific example in your life, describe the situation.

2. Describe a situation in which you were mentally ready for a challenge because you had developed mental toughness.

*3. What request by the apostle Paul indicates he was

determined to stay mentally tough even while in prison?
See 2 Timothy 4:13.

4. What could be considered danger signals that indicate
    you are a fast starter, a personal quality you have
    considered a positive benefit until now?

5. What provides you with the mental stimulation you know
    you should be getting, but you have not given it priority?
    a. Specific reading to enlarge your base of information
    b. Professional seminars that enrich and challenge your
        thinking
    c. A mentor or close friend who consistently challenges
        your thinking
    d. Other

    _____

    _____

    _____

    _____

    _____

    _____

6. What percentage of your reading or your interaction with
    others challenges your status quo? Name two books you
    have read with which you disagreed.

    a. _____

    b. _____

*7. List some of the indicators of mental toughness in Paul's address to the Athenians in Acts 17:16–32.

_____

_____

_____

_____

8. The author writes, "The best kind of thinking is accomplished when it is done in the context of reverence for God's kingly reign over all creation." What kind of preparation will you need to do to develop that context?

9. A Presbyterian pastor annually speaks and fields questions at a local "skeptics corner" attended by unbelievers only. This heavy interaction with the non-Christian mind sharpens his awareness of the Enemy's tactics. What can you do to achieve a similar result?

*10. What are some of the non-Christian ideas we can fall prey to when our minds become dull?

11. What are some areas of your thought life that need expanding and toughening? Beside each area, list a resource that you can tap to help you.

_____

_____

_____

_____

CHAPTER 9: THE SADNESS OF
A BOOK NEVER READ

*1. The author suggests we need to learn to think Christianly. What does that mean?

2. If you did not have the advantage of growing up in a strongly Christian environment, what can you do to "catch up"?

3. In what parts of your world can you learn to "appreciate the messages God has written in creation"?

*4. What can you do to enhance your storehouse of information, ideas, and insights?

5. List the three steps in becoming a listener. Then describe what you can do to personalize these steps in your listening process.

   a. _____

   b. _____

   c. _____

6. Describe a situation in which listening to God or to another person helped you take a major step forward.

7. What book have you wanted to read for a long time but haven't done so as yet? When can you get it into your schedule?

8. What set Ezra apart from other leaders of his day? Turn to Psalm 119:33–40 and describe the characteristics of this kind of student.

*9. What are your obstacles to beginning a program of offensive study if you do not already have one?

*10. What areas should we as Christians study intensively if we are to make a significant difference in our world?

11. What area of offensive study do you need to begin if you are to achieve excellence as a servant in your position? List the top resource that you need to acquire to do so.

_____

_____

CHAPTER 10: ORDER IN THE GARDEN

1. If you were confined to a prisoner-of-war camp without a Bible, how effective would you be in recalling Scripture? What can you do to learn more Scripture?

2. If you were totally honest with yourself, how would you describe your inner communion with God?

3. The author writes, "If we are ever to develop a spiritual life that gives contentment, it will be because we approach spiritual living as a discipline, much as the athlete trains his body for competition." Do you agree or disagree? If you disagree, write out your reasons.

4. What are some of the metaphors you would use to describe your inner spiritual center?

5. Write out the privileges we lose if we do not have a disciplined approach to inner spiritual development. Now check off those you sense are missing in your life.

a. _____

b. _____

c. _____

d. _____

6. What pressure situations in life helped you begin the development of your inner spiritual life?

7. What is the deepest desire of your heart for your inner life with God? What can you do to have that desire satisfied?

*8. What did David gain from his communion with God, as described in Psalm 27?

CHAPTER 11: NO OUTER PROPS NECESSARY

1. If you were to be left helpless by a physical disability, where would you turn for the strength to survive?

2. What was the secret of E. Stanley Jones's serenity when he was disabled by a stroke?

3. Write out the five spiritual exercises recommended as critical and give yourself a rating from 1 to 10 on each (with 10 as the best).

a. _____

b. _____

c. _____

d. _____

e. _____

4. Describe some of the noisy intrusions in your life that rob you of the silence and solitude the author recommends.

*5. What can we learn from the silence/solitude of Zacharias; his wife, Elizabeth; and Mary, the mother of Jesus?

6. The author describes the difficulties in quieting the inner self to attain solitude. Try it and write down the results.

*7. What aids do you employ to listen to God in your private world?

8. What is the key contribution of a personal journal?

9. What are some of the things the author records in his journal?

10. Use this space to make your first journal entry if you have not yet started journaling. Let it be your experiment.

_____

_____

_____

_____

_____

_____

CHAPTER 12: EVERYTHING HAS TO BE ENTERED

1. Describe a time in your life when neither the inner strands nor the outer props were strong enough to hold you up. If you have not had such an experience, describe how you avoided such a time.

*2. Describe an experience you or someone you know has had that is similar to that of Samuel in the Old Testament.

3. What does the author call the Enter key for effective internalization of what we hear in silence and solitude?

4. What happens in meditation, according to the author?

5. Stop to meditate on your favorite psalm. If you do not have one, take time with Psalm 139.

6. The author writes, "We often enter the chamber to meet with God while we are still emotionally out of breath." If this has happened to you, what can you do to prevent it in the future?

*7. List the two great Christian classics that you want to read during the next six months.

a. _____

b. _____

8. How can you use your imagination to enrich your meditation? Return to the psalm you read meditatively earlier and reread it with an active imagination. Write down some of your thoughts.

CHAPTER 13: SEEING THROUGH HEAVEN'S EYES

*1. How did the attitude of the saints of the past differ from their contemporaries, according to Bridget Herman? If you know someone with the same attitude, describe your experience with that person.

2. Write down reasons why we have trouble praying. Personalize the one that troubles you the most by writing out a prayer of confession expressing your feelings.

3. What does the author suggest as a reason for the greater

ease with which women pray in public? If you are a
married man, make this a journal entry about your
attitudes and feelings about praying with your wife.

*4. What is a sign of significant spiritual growth, according
   to the author?

5. Make a journal entry describing your frustration with
   unanswered prayer.

6. What prayer is among the purest we can pray?

7. Why does the author keep a prayer list?

8. Write out a prayer expression of adoration.

9. If you were to confess to some of the sin "boulders" in
   your life, what would they be?

10. What are the twelve "apostles of ill health," according to
    E. Stanley Jones?

*11. If you were to visualize yourself as an intercessory prayer
    warrior, how would you describe your prayer life?

12. What was the secret of the extraordinary leadership
    power of Eric Liddell, the missionary-prisoner?

13. Write out the deepest desire of your heart in respect to
    prayer.

CHAPTER 14: FRIENDS

1. The author describes the "Capital-F Friends" of his
   adulthood. What qualities do they have? Do you have any
   Capital-F Friends of your own?

2. How does having a circle of Capital-F Friends help you
   order your private world?

3. If you have trusted friends in your life, how can you
   show them your appreciation? If you do not have trusted
   friends, how would you go about recruiting some?

4. Try to describe some famous biblical friendships. What

were the qualities of those friendships, and how did they serve and protect the people involved?

CHAPTER 15: REST BEYOND LEISURE (SABBATHING)

1. What does *sabbathing* mean to you? Is it active or passive? How does the author's use of *sabbath* as a verb possibly alter its meaning?
2. Consider Jesus' tendency to withdraw from others for prayer. What else did He accomplish during His rest? How did it equip Him for the demands on Him? See Mark 1:35–39.
*3. How did God "close the loop" on His creation activity?
*4. What is the foremost purpose for the rest instituted by God?
5. Are you experiencing the "rest that reaffirms truth"? If you are not, what steps do you need to take to make it happen?
6. What do you need to do to experience the kind of rest that redefines your mission in life?
*7. What is the content of sabbath rest, according to the author?
8. What personal sabbath-rest plan could be possible for you and your spouse?
9. Make a journal entry of the key ideas/concepts you have absorbed from reading and studying this book. Then add some of the exciting developments as you have implemented recommended action.

NOTES

AUTHOR'S NOTE

1. Oswald Chambers, "Where the Battle's Lost and Won," *My Utmost for His Highest*, accessed April 17, 2016, https://utmost.org/classic/where-the-battle%E2%80%99s-lost-and-won-classic/.

CHAPTER 1: THE SINKHOLE SYNDROME

1. William Barclay, *The Letters to the Galatians and Ephesians* (Philadelphia: Westminster, 1976), 100.
2. Wayne Muller, *Sabbath: Finding Rest, Renewal, and Delight in Our Busy Lives* (New York: Bantam Doubleday Dell, 2000), 2.
3. Anne Morrow Lindbergh, *The Gift from the Sea* (New York: Pantheon, 1955), 23–24.
4. Dorothie Bobbe, *Abigail Adams* (New York: Putnam, 1966), 206.

CHAPTER 2: A VIEW FROM THE BRIDGE

1. "Executive's Crisis," *Wall Street Journal*, March 12, 1982, 1.
2. James Buchan, *The Indomitable Mary Slessor* (New York: Seabury, 1981), 86.
3. Ralph Waldo Emerson, *Self-Reliance and Other Essays* (Mineola, NY: Dover Publications, 1993), 23.

CHAPTER 3: CAUGHT IN A GOLDEN CAGE
1. Stephen R. Covey, *Principle-Centered Leadership* (New York: Free Press, 1991).

CHAPTER 4: THE TRAGIC TALE OF A SUCCESSFUL LOSER
1. Paul Tournier, *Creative Suffering* (New York: Harper & Row, 1983).

CHAPTER 5: LIVING AS A CALLED PERSON
1. Cardinal Danneels of Brussels, quoted in Jean Vanier, *Community and Growth* (Mahwah, NJ: Paulist Press, 1989), 210.
2. Herbert Butterfield, *Christianity and History* (New York: Charles Scribner's Sons, 1949), 115.

CHAPTER 6: HAS ANYONE SEEN MY TIME? I'VE MISPLACED IT!
1. William Barclay, *The Gospel of Matthew* (Philadelphia: Westminster, 1975), 280.

CHAPTER 7: RECAPTURING MY TIME
1. Elton Trueblood, *While It Is Day* (New York: Harper & Row, 1974), 67.
2. Harold Begbie, *Life of General William Booth* (New York: MacMillan, 1920), 178.
3. C. S. Lewis, *Letters to an American Lady* (Grand Rapids: Eerdmans, 1975), 53.

CHAPTER 8: THE BETTER MAN LOST
1. David Denby, *Great Books* (New York: Simon & Schuster, 1997), 15.
2. Elton Trueblood, *While It Is Day* (New York: Harper & Row, 1974), 97–98.
3. Oliver Wendell Holmes, *Speeches* (Boston: Little, Brown, 1891), 43.
4. Norman Polmar and Thomas B. Allen, *Rickover: Controversy and Genius* (New York: Simon & Schuster, 1982), 267.
5. Oswald Chambers, *Leagues of Light: Diary of Oswald Chambers 1915–1917* (Louisville, KY: Operation Appreciation Ministries, 1984), 42.

CHAPTER 9: THE SADNESS OF A BOOK NEVER READ

1. Ernest Dimnet, *The Art of Thinking* (New York: Simon & Schuster, 1928), 33.

CHAPTER 10: ORDER IN THE GARDEN

1. Howard Rutledge and Phyllis Rutledge with Mel White and Lyla White, *In the Presence of Mine Enemies* (Old Tappan, NY: Fleming Revell, 1973), 34.
2. Brother Lawrence, Seventh Letter, *The Practice of the Presence of God*, trans. E. M. Blaiklock (Nashville: Thomas Nelson, 1982).
3. Thomas Kelly, quoted in Richard Foster, *Freedom of Simplicity* (New York: Harper & Row, 1981), 78; Thomas Kelly, *A Testament of Devotion* (New York: Harper & Row Publishers, 1941), 115.

CHAPTER 11: NO OUTER PROPS NECESSARY

1. E. Stanley Jones, *The Divine Yes* (Nashville: Abingdon, 1975), 63.
2. Malcolm Muggeridge, *Something Beautiful for God* (Garden City, NY: Image, 1977), 48.
3. Henri J. M. Nouwen, *The Way of the Heart* (New York: Seabury, 1981), 39.
4. Wayne E. Oates, *Nurturing Silence in a Noisy Heart* (Garden City, NY: Doubleday, 1979), 3.
5. Matthew Bridges, "Crown Him with Many Crowns" (1851) with music by George Job Elvey.
6. Thomas Chisholm, "Great Is Thy Faithfulness" (1923) with music by William M. Runyan.
7. William R. Featherstone, "My Jesus, I Love Thee" (1864) with music by Adoniram J. Gordon.
8. Fanny J. Crosby, "Rescue the Perishing" (1869) with music by William H. Doane.
9. Eliza E. Hewitt, "When We All Get to Heaven" (1898) with music by Emily D. Wilson.
10. Carl Boberg, trans. by Stuart Hine, "How Great Thou Art" (1949).
11. J. Wilbur Chapman, "One Day" (1910) with music by Charles H. Marsh.

12. Harry D. Clarke, "Into My Heart" (1924).
13. William Zinsser, *Writing to Learn* (New York: Harper & Row, 1988), 16.
14. C. Austin Miles, "In the Garden" (1913).

CHAPTER 12: EVERYTHING HAS TO BE ENTERED

1. E. Stanley Jones, *A Song of Ascents* (Nashville: Abingdon Press, 1968), 104.
2. Clarence W. Hall, *Samuel Logan Brengle: Portrait of a Prophet* (Chicago: Salvation Army Supply & Purchasing Dept., 1933), 185.
3. John Baillie, *A Diary of Private Prayer* (New York: Charles Scribner's Sons, 1949), 27.
4. C. S. Lewis, *Letters to an American Lady* (Grand Rapids: Eerdmans, 1975), 73.

CHAPTER 13: SEEING THROUGH HEAVEN'S EYES

1. Bridget Herman, *Creative Prayer* (Cincinnati: Forward Movement, n.d.), 16.
2. Thomas Kelly, *A Testament of Devotion* (New York: Harper & Row, 1941), 39.
3. Brother Lawrence, *The Practice of the Presence of God*, trans. E. M. Blaiklock (Nashville: Thomas Nelson, 1982), 70.
4. Henri J. M. Nouwen, *Clowning in Rome* (Garden City, NY: Image, 1979), 73.
5. Kelly, *A Testament of Devotion*, 54.
6. Clarence W. Hall, *Samuel Logan Brengle: Portrait of a Prophet* (Chicago: Salvation Army Supply & Purchasing Dept., 1933), 237.
7. Ibid.
8. E. Stanley Jones, *A Song of Ascents* (Nashville: Abingdon Press, 1968), 337.
9. Hall, *Samuel Logan Brengle*, 185.
10. Sally Magnusson, *The Flying Scotsman* (New York: Quartet Books, 1981), 165.

CHAPTER 14: FRIENDS

1. John Pollock, *Hudson Taylor and Maria* (London: Hodder and Stoughton, 1963).
2. Edward Farrell, quoted in Margaret Magdalen, *Jesus Man of Prayer* (Downers Grove, IL: Intervarsity, 1987).

CHAPTER 15: REST BEYOND LEISURE (SABBATHING)

1. Brother Lawrence, *The Practice of the Presence of God*, trans. E. M. Blaiklock (Nashville: Thomas Nelson, 1982), 85.
2. Robert Robinson, "Come, Thou Fount of Every Blessing" (1758).
3. Abraham Heschel, *The Earth Is the Lord's* and *The Sabbath* (two books published as one, New York: Harper Torchbooks, 1966), 10.
4. Hugh Evan Hopkins, *Charles Simeon of Cambridge* (Grand Rapids: Eerdmans, 1977), 155–56.
5. Robert Isaac Wilberforce and Samuel Wilberforce, *The Life of William Wilberforce* (London: Seeley, Burnside, and Seeley, 1843), 270.

EPILOGUE: COURAGE, APPRECIATION, DEPTH

1. Psalm 46:1–3 NIV.

ABOUT THE AUTHOR

GORDON MACDONALD HAS BEEN A PASTOR AND AUTHOR FOR MORE than fifty years. He presently serves as chancellor at Denver Seminary and is a speaker at leadership conferences around the world. His books include *Building Below the Waterline, Who Stole My Church?*, and *A Resilient Life*. Gordon and his wife, Gail, live in New Hampshire.